Foreword

A decade of intense combat in two theaters has taught us many lessons about what works and what does not in the effort to accomplish that all-important mission of saving lives in battle. A severely injured Soldier today has about twice the likelihood of surviving his wounds compared to Soldiers in wars as recent as Vietnam. That progress is the result of many things: better tactics and weapons, better body armor and helmets, better trained and fitter Soldiers. But, the introduction of Tactical Combat Casualty Care (TCCC) throughout the Army has certainly been an important part of that improvement.

TCCC is fundamentally different from civilian care. It is the thoughtful integration of tactics and medicine, but to make it work takes a different set of skills and equipment, and every Soldier and leader needs to understand it and practice it.

This handbook is the result of years of careful study of the care of wounded Soldiers, painstaking research by medics and physicians, and the ability of leaders at all levels to see and understand the lessons being learned and the willingness to make the changes in equipment, training, and doctrine needed to improve the performance of the Army Health System. It is the best guidance we have at the time of publication, but new information, new techniques, or new equipment will drive changes in the future. Be assured that these performance improvement efforts will continue as long as American Soldiers go in harm's way.

JAMES W. KIRKPATRICK, MD
COL (ret), MC
Senior Clinical Consultant
Directorate of Combat and Doctrine Development
AMEDD Center & School

Tactical Combat Casualty Care Handbook
Table of Contents

Chapter 1. Tactical Combat Casualty Care
- Section I: Introduction
- Section II: Care Under Fire
- Section III: Tactical Field Care
- Section IV: Tactical Evacuation Care
- Section V: Management Guidelines

Chapter 2. Tactical Combat Casualty Care Procedures
- Section I: Hemorrhage Control
- Section II: Airway Management
- Section III: Breathing Management
- Section IV: Vascular Access
- Section V: Hypothermia Prevention
- Section VI: Medication Considerations

Appendix A. Triage Categories

Appendix B. Medical Evacuation Request

Appendix C. Medical Evacuation Precedence Categories

Appendix D. Roles of Medical Care

Appendix E. Combat Wound Pack

Appendix F. Improved First Aid Kit

Appendix G. Warrior Aid and Litter Kit

Appendix H. Aid Bag Considerations

Appendix I. National Stock Numbers

Appendix J. References and Resources

CENTER FOR ARMY LESSONS LEARNED

Center For Army Lessons Learned	
Director	COL Thomas H. Roe
Division Chief	LTC Vaughn M. Grizzle
CALL Analyst	Donald Haus
Chief Author	MAJ (Retired) Jeffrey Mott, DHSc, PA-C
Contributing Authors	Brian Hill, PhD, PA-C
	LTC (Retired) Donald Parson, MPAS, PA-C
Center for Predeployment Medicine	
Subject Matter Expert Consultants	
	CPT Larry Ake, MPAS, PA-C
	MAJ Joseph Dominguez III, MPAS, PA-C
	MAJ Felipe Galvan, MPAS, PA-C
	MAJ (ret) Mark Geslak, MPAS, PA-C
	CPT Michael Holloway, MPAS, PA-C
	CPT Donald Merrill, MPAS, PA-C
	CPT Miguel Moran, MPAS, PA-C
	MAJ (Retired) Bret Smith, MPAS, PA-C

CALL wishes to acknowledge the Army Medical Department Center and School's Center for Predeployment Medicine, the Committee on Tactical Combat Casualty Care, and the Army Institute of Surgical Research for their roles in compiling this handbook.

The Secretary of the Army has determined that the publication of this periodical is necessary in the transaction of the public business as required by law of the Department.

Unless otherwise stated, whenever the masculine or feminine gender is used, both are intended.

Note: Any publications (other than CALL publications) referenced in this product, such as ARs, FMs, and TMs, must be obtained through your pinpoint distribution system.

Chapter 1
Tactical Combat Casualty Care
Section I: Introduction

Tactical Combat Casualty Care (TCCC) is the prehospital care rendered to a casualty in a tactical, combat environment. The principles of TCCC are fundamentally different from those of traditional civilian trauma care, which is practiced by most medical providers and medics. These differences are based on both the unique patterns and types of wounds that are suffered in combat and the tactical environment medical personnel face in combat. Unique combat wounds and tactical environments make it difficult to determine which intervention to perform at what time. Besides addressing a casualty's medical condition, responding medical personnel must also address the tactical situation faced while providing casualty care in combat. A medically correct intervention performed at the wrong time may lead to further casualties. Stated another way, "good medicine may be bad tactics,"[1] which can get the rescuer and casualty killed. To successfully navigate these issues, medical providers must have skills and training focused on combat trauma care, as opposed to civilian trauma care.

Casualties and Wounds

On the battlefield, the prehospital period is the most important time to care for any combat casualty. In previous wars, up to 90 percent of combat deaths occurred before a casualty reached a medical treatment facility. This highlights the primary importance of treating battlefield casualties at the point of injury, prior to tactical evacuation care and arrival at a treatment facility.

Specifically, combat deaths result from the following:[2]

- 31 percent: Penetrating head trauma.
- 25 percent: Surgically uncorrectable torso trauma.
- 10 percent: Potentially correctable surgical trauma.
- **9 percent: Exsanguination.***
- 7 percent: Mutilating blast trauma.

- **3-4 percent: Tension pneumothorax (PTX).***
- **2 percent: Airway obstruction/injury.***
- 5 percent: Died of wounds (mainly infection and shock).

*Potentially Survivable

(**Note:** Numbers do not add up to 100 percent. Not all causes of death are listed. Some deaths are due to multiple causes.)

A significant percentage of these deaths (highlighted above in bold type) are potentially survivable with proper, timely intervention. Of these avoidable deaths, the vast majority are due to exsanguination and airway or breathing difficulties, conditions that can and should be addressed at the point of injury. It has been estimated that of all potentially survivable deaths, up to 90 percent of them can be avoided with the simple application of a tourniquet for extremity hemorrhage, the rapid treatment of a PTX, and the establishment of a stable airway.[3]

On the battlefield, casualties will fall into three general categories:

- Casualties who will live, regardless of receiving any medical aid.
- Casualties who will die, regardless of receiving any medical aid.
- Casualties who will die if they do not receive timely and appropriate medical aid.

TCCC addresses the third category of casualties — those who require the most attention of the medical provider during combat.

TCCC versus Advanced Trauma Life Support

Prior to the Global War on Terrorism, trauma care training for military medical personnel traditionally was based on the principles of the civilian Emergency Medical Technicians Basic Course and basic and advanced trauma life support (ATLS). These principles, especially ATLS, provide a standardized and very successful approach to the management of civilian trauma patients in a hospital setting. However, some of these principles may not apply in the civilian prehospital setting, let alone in a tactical, combat environment.[4]

The prehospital phase of casualty care is the most critical phase of care for combat casualties, accounting for up to 90 percent of combat deaths. Furthermore, combat casualties can suffer from potentially devastating injuries not usually seen in the civilian setting. Most casualties during combat are the result of penetrating injuries, rather than the blunt trauma seen in the civilian setting. Combat casualties may also suffer massive, complex trauma, including traumatic limb amputation and penetrating chest wounds. In addition to the medical differences between civilian and combat trauma, several other factors affect casualty care in combat, including the following:

- Hostile fire may be present, preventing treatment of the casualty.
- Medical equipment is limited to that carried by mission personnel.
- Tactical considerations may dictate that mission completion take precedence over casualty care.
- Time until evacuation is highly variable (from minutes to hours or days).
- Rapid evacuation may not be possible based on the tactical situation.

TCCC Goals

TCCC presents a system to manage combat casualties that takes the issues discussed above into consideration. The guiding principle of TCCC is performing the correct intervention at the correct time in the continuum of field care. TCCC is ultimately structured to meet three important goals:

- Treat the casualty.
- Prevent additional casualties.
- Complete the mission.

Stages of Care

In thinking about the management of combat casualties, it is helpful to divide care into three distinct phases, each with its own characteristics and limitations:

- **Care under fire** is the care rendered at the point of injury while both the medic and the casualty are under effective hostile fire. The risk of additional injuries from hostile fire at any moment is extremely high for both the casualty and the medic. Available medical equipment is limited to that carried by the medic and the casualty.
- **Tactical field care** is the care rendered by the medic once he and the casualty are no longer under effective hostile fire. It also applies to situations in which an injury has occurred on a mission but there has been no hostile fire. Available medical equipment is still limited to that carried into the field by mission personnel. Time to evacuation may vary from minutes to hours.

- **Tactical evacuation care** is the care rendered once the casualty has been picked up by an aircraft, vehicle, or boat. Additional medical personnel and equipment that has been pre-staged in these assets should be available during this phase of casualty management.

The chapters and sections of this handbook will present a discussion of each stage of TCCC as well as instructions for the procedures TCCC requires.

Section II: Care Under Fire

Care under fire is the care rendered by the rescuer at the point of injury while he and the casualty are still under effective hostile fire. The risk of additional injuries at any moment is extremely high for both the casualty and the rescuer. The major considerations during this phase of care are the following:

- Suppression of hostile fire.
- Moving the casualty to a safe position.
- Treatment of immediate life-threatening hemorrhage.

Casualty care during the care under fire phase is complicated by several tactical factors. First, the medical equipment available for care is limited to that carried by the individual Soldiers and the rescuers. Second, the unit's personnel may be engaged with hostile forces and, especially in small-unit engagements, may not be available to assist with casualty treatment and evacuation. Third, the tactical situation often prevents the medic or medical provider from performing a detailed examination or definitive treatment of casualties. Furthermore, these situations often occur during night operations, resulting in severe visual limitations while treating the casualty.

Defensive Actions

The rapid success of the combat mission is the immediate priority and the best way to prevent the risk of injury to other personnel or additional injuries to casualties. Medical personnel carry small arms to defend themselves and casualties in the field. The additional firepower from the medical personnel may be essential to obtaining fire superiority. Initially, medical personnel may need to assist in returning fire before stopping to care for the casualty. Additionally, casualties who have sustained non-life-threatening injuries and are still able to participate in the fight after self aid, must continue to return fire as they are able.

As soon as the rescuer is directed or able, his first major objective is to keep the casualty from sustaining additional injuries. Wounded Soldiers who are unable to participate further in the engagement should lay flat and still if no ground cover is available, or move as quickly as possible if nearby cover is available. The medic may be able to direct the injured Soldier to nearby cover and provide self-aid.

Airway Management

Do not perform any immediate management of the airway during the care under fire phase. Airway injuries typically play a minimal role in combat casualties, comprising only 1 to 2 percent of casualties primarily from maxillofacial trauma. The primary concern is to move the casualty to cover as quickly as possible. The time, equipment, and positioning required to manage an impaired airway expose the casualty and rescuer to increased risk. Rescuers should defer airway management until the tactical field care phase, when the casualty and rescuer are safe from direct hostile fire.

Hemorrhage Control

The number one potentially survivable cause of death on the battlefield is hemorrhage from a compressible wound. Therefore, the primary medical interventions during the care under fire phase are directed toward stopping any life-threatening bleeding as quickly as possible. Injuries to an artery or other major vessel can rapidly result in hemorrhagic shock and exsanguinations. A casualty may exsanguinate before medical help arrives, so definitive control of life-threatening hemorrhage on the battlefield cannot be overemphasized. In Vietnam, bleeding from an extremity wound was the cause of death in more than 2,500 casualties who had sustained no other injury.[5] This held to be true after a decade of post-September 11, 2001, combat where more than 90 percent of 4,596 service members died of hemorrhage-associated injuries.[6]

Extremity wounds. The rapid, temporary use of a tourniquet is the recommended management for all life-threatening extremity hemorrhages.[7] Standard field dressings and direct pressure may not work reliably to control an extremity hemorrhage. While traditional ATLS training discourages the use of tourniquets, they are appropriate in the tactical combat setting. The benefits of tourniquet use over other methods of hemorrhage control include:

- Direct pressure and compression are difficult to perform and maintain in combat settings and result in delays in getting the rescuer and casualty to cover.

- Tourniquets can be applied to the casualty by himself, thus limiting the rescuer's exposure to hostile fire.

- There are few complications from tourniquet use. Ischemic damage is rare if the tourniquet is in place for less than two hours.

During the care under fire phase, the casualty and rescuer remain in grave danger from hostile fire. If the casualty is observed to have bleeding from an extremity, the care provider should apply a hasty tourniquet to the injured extremity over the uniform, as high on the extremity as possible, and move the casualty to cover as quickly as possible.[8]

Nonextremity wounds. These injuries are difficult to treat in the care under fire phase. Attempt to provide direct pressure to these wounds as you rapidly move the casualty to cover. Once under cover, hemostatic agents with an overwrapped pressure dressing or a mechanical junctional hemorrhage control device are appropriate for these injuries.

Casualty Transportation

Transportation of the casualty is often the most problematic aspect of TCCC. In the care under fire phase, transportation is complicated by the limited equipment and personnel available and the risk of further injury due to hostile fire. Removing the casualty from the field of fire as quickly as possible is the transportation priority during this phase of care.[9] Do not attempt to save a casualty's rucksack unless it contains items that are critical to the mission. However, if at all possible, take the casualty's weapons and ammunition. The enemy may use them against you.

Cervical spine immobilization. Although the civilian standard of care is to immobilize the cervical spinal column prior to moving a patient with injuries that might have resulted in damage to the spine, this practice is generally not appropriate in the combat setting. In Vietnam, studies examining the value of cervical spinal immobilization in penetrating neck injuries found that only 1.4 percent of casualties with penetrating neck injuries would have possibly benefited from immobilization of the cervical spine.[10] The time required to accomplish cervical spine immobilization was found to be 5.5 minutes, even when using experienced rescuers. More recent research showed a 0.6 percent spinal cord involvement and spinal immobilization in penetrating trauma as falling out of favor even in civilian emergency medicine.[11] In addition, the equipment needed for this procedure (long spine board) is generally not available at the point of injury. Therefore, the potential hazards of hostile fire to both the casualty and rescuer outweigh the potential benefit of cervical spine immobilization. However, for casualties with significant blunt trauma, cervical spine immobilization is appropriate during the care under fire phase. Motor vehicle rollovers, parachuting or fast-roping injuries, falls greater than 15 feet, and other types of trauma resulting in neck pain or unconsciousness should be treated with spinal immobilization, unless the danger of hostile fire constitutes a greater risk in the judgment of the medic.

Transportation methods. Standard litters for patient evacuation may not be available for movement of casualties in the care under fire phase. Consider using alternate methods of evacuation, such as dragging the casualty out of the field of fire by his body armor. There are a number of commercially fabricated drag straps and drag litters available to help expedite this move, or one can be improvised by using 1-inch tubular nylon. Traditional one- and two-man carries are not recommended as the weight of the average combatant makes these types of casualty movement techniques extremely difficult. Additionally, consider the use of obscurants such as smoke or CS (irritating agent) to assist in casualty recovery. Vehicles can also be used as a screen during recovery attempts. In Iraq, there were several reported instances of tanks being used as screens to facilitate a casualty evacuation from care under fire.

Section III: Tactical Field Care

Tactical field care is the care rendered to the casualty once the casualty and rescuer are no longer under effective hostile fire. This term also applies to situations where an injury has occurred on a mission but there has been no hostile fire. This phase of care is characterized by the following:

- The risk from hostile fire has been reduced but still exists.
- The medical equipment available is still limited by what has been brought into the field by mission personnel.
- The time available for treatment is highly variable. Time prior to evacuation or re-engagement with hostile forces can range from a few minutes to many hours.

Medical care during this phase of care is directed toward more in-depth evaluation and treatment of the casualty, focusing on those conditions not addressed during the care under fire phase of treatment. The casualty and rescuer are now in a somewhat less hazardous situation, a setting more appropriate for a rapid trauma assessment and treatment. However, evaluation and treatment are still dictated by the tactical situation.

In some cases, tactical field care will consist of rapid treatment of wounds with the expectation of a re-engagement with hostile forces at any moment. The need to avoid undertaking nonessential evaluation and treatment is critical in such cases. Conversely, care may be rendered once the mission has reached an anticipated evacuation point without pursuit and is awaiting evacuation. In these circumstances, there may be ample time to render whatever care is feasible in the field. However, as time to evacuation may vary greatly, medical providers and medics must take care to partition supplies and equipment in the event of prolonged evacuation wait times.

Cardiopulmonary Resuscitation (CPR)

In casualties of blast or penetrating injury, found to be without pulse, respiration, or other signs of life, CPR on the battlefield will generally not be successful and should not be attempted. Attempts to resuscitate trauma patients in arrest have been found to be futile even in urban settings where victims are in close proximity to trauma centers. On the battlefield, the cost of performing CPR on casualties with what are inevitably fatal injuries will result in additional lives lost, because care is withheld from casualties with less severe injuries. Also, these attempts expose rescuers to additional hazards from hostile fire. Prior to the tactical evacuation care phase, rescuers should consider CPR only in the cases of nontraumatic disorders such as hypothermia, near drowning, or electrocution.[12]

Altered Mental Status

Immediately disarm any casualty with an altered mental status, including secondary weapons and explosive devices. An armed combatant with an altered mental status is a significant risk to himself and those in his unit. The four main reasons for an altered mental status are traumatic brain injury (TBI), pain, shock, and analgesic medication (for example, morphine or ketamine).

Hemorrhage Control

Compressible hemorrhage is the leading potentially survivable cause of death on the battlefield. In the tactical field care phase, hemorrhage control includes addressing any significant bleeding sites not previously controlled. When evaluating the casualty for bleeding sites, remove only the amount of clothing needed to expose and treat injuries. Ensure the transition zones are free of injury and allow for a deliberate tourniquet(s) to be placed against the skin.[13] If necessary, stop significant extremity bleeding as quickly as possible using a tourniquet without hesitation, if the injury is amenable to its use. In the event that the injury is too high on an extremity and not amenable to a tourniquet, use of a mechanical junctional hemorrhage control device is appropriate in the tactical field care phase.[14]

It is important to note that after tourniquet application, a distal pulse must be assessed to ensure that arterial blood flow has been stopped. If a distal pulse remains after tourniquet application, then a second tourniquet must be applied side by side, touching, and just above the original tourniquet. This second tourniquet applies pressure over a wider area and more effectively stops the arterial blood flow. After the successful application of a deliberate tourniquet(s), the hasty tourniquet placed during care under fire may be removed.[15]

There have been a number of reports of compartment syndrome in distal extremities when the tourniquet is not applied tightly enough to stop arterial blood flow. In addition, there have been tourniquet failures when the care provider has attempted to tighten the tourniquet to the extreme. If a tourniquet is applied around the limb as snugly as possible before the windlass is tightened, it should only take three, 180-degree revolutions (540 degrees total) of the windlass to stop blood flow.[16] If a distal pulse is still present, it is more prudent to apply a second tourniquet as described above than to try tightening the original one too tightly. It must be pointed out that the additional step of checking a distal pulse should only be performed when the tactical situation permits.

Tourniquets should remain in place until the casualty has been transported to the evacuation point. Once the patient has been transported to the site where evacuation is anticipated, and any time the casualty is moved, reassess any tourniquets previously applied. If evacuation is significantly delayed (greater than two hours), the medic should determine if the tourniquet should be loosened and bleeding control replaced with some other technique. Hemostatic gauze, pressure bandages, etc., may control the bleeding and lower the risk to the extremity that a tourniquet poses. However, it needs to be emphasized that there is no evidence that tourniquets have caused the loss of any limbs in thousands of tourniquet applications.[17] If a decision to remove a tourniquet is made, the medic must be sure to complete any required fluid resuscitation prior to tourniquet discontinuation. It is not necessary to remove the tourniquet; the medic only needs to loosen it. This allows the tourniquet to be reapplied if the hemorrhage cannot be controlled by other methods.

Data from research done in theater have demonstrated that applying a tourniquet before the casualty goes into shock significantly improves survival statistics. The training emphasis must continue to be on the control of bleeding in all casualties.

Breathing

The second potentially survivable cause of death on the battlefield is breathing problems, specifically the development of a tension PTX. Traumatic defects in the casualty's chest wall may result in an open PTX. All penetrating chest wounds should be treated as such by covering the wound during expiration with an occlusive dressing. Multiple commercial chest seals are now available with excellent adhesive properties, but improvised occlusive seals with tape are adequate. The dressing should be sealed on all edges.[18] The casualty should then be placed in a sitting position, if applicable, and monitored for the development of a tension PTX that should be treated as described below.

Tension PTX. Assume any progressive, severe respiratory distress on the battlefield resulting from penetrating chest trauma represents a tension PTX. Do not rely on such typical signs as breath sounds, tracheal shift, jugular vein distention, and hyper-resonance on percussion for diagnosis in this setting because these signs may not always be present. Even if these signs are present, they may be difficult to detect on the battlefield. Treat tension PTXs in the tactical field care phase via decompression with a 14-gauge, 3.25-inch-long needle with catheter.[19] A casualty with penetrating chest trauma will generally have some degree of hemothorax or PTX as a result of the wound. The additional trauma caused by a needle thoracostomy will not worsen the condition in the absence of a tension PTX. Decompress the casualty by inserting the needle with catheter into the second intercostals space at the midclavicular line, ensuring the needle is not medial to the nipple line. Remove the needle and leave the catheter buried to the hub. An acceptable alternate site is the fourth or fifth intercostals space at the anterior axillary line;[20] ensure to position the casualty with the affected side up in the event of an accompanying hemothorax.

The medic must monitor this casualty after the procedure to ensure that the catheter has not clotted or dislodged and respiratory symptoms have not returned. If respiratory symptoms have returned or the catheter is clotted or dislodged, flush the catheter or perform a second needle thoracostomy adjacent to the first. Chest tubes are not recommended during this phase of care because they are not needed for initial treatment of a tension PTX, are more technically difficult and time-consuming to perform, and are more likely to result in additional tissue damage and subsequent infection.

Airway Management

Airway compromise is the third potentially survivable cause of death on the battlefield. In the tactical field care phase, management and treatment of the casualty's airway is performed after all hemorrhage and penetrating chest trauma have been addressed. In the event of significant maxillofacial trauma or inhalation burns, airway compromise should be addressed prior to penetrating chest trauma. Intervention should proceed from the least invasive procedure to the most invasive. Do not attempt any airway intervention if the casualty is conscious and breathing well on his own. Allow the casualty to assume the most comfortable position that best protects his airway, to include sitting upright.

Unconscious casualty without airway obstruction. If the casualty is unconscious, the most likely cause is either hemorrhagic shock or head trauma. In either case, an adequate airway must be maintained. If the unconscious casualty does not exhibit signs of airway obstruction, the airway should first be opened with a chin lift or a jaw-thrust maneuver. As in the care under fire phase, cervical spine immobilization is generally not required, except when the mechanism of injury involves significant blunt trauma.

If spontaneous respirations are present without respiratory distress, an adequate airway in the unconscious casualty is best maintained with a nasopharyngeal airway (NPA). An NPA is preferred over an oropharyngeal airway because it is better tolerated if the casualty regains consciousness and it is less likely to be dislodged during casualty transport. After inserting the NPA, place the casualty in the recovery position (see Figure 1-1) to maintain the open airway and prevent aspiration of blood, mucous, or vomit.

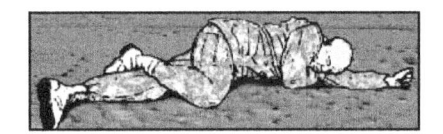

Figure 1-1. Recovery position

Current or impending airway obstruction. For casualties with a current or impending airway obstruction, the initial intervention is again to open the airway with either a chin lift or a jaw-thrust maneuver. Either maneuver is followed by the insertion of an NPA. However, if an airway obstruction develops or persists despite the use of an NPA, a more definitive airway is required. In casualties with significant maxillofacial trauma or inhalation burns, a more definitive airway, such as a surgical cricothyroidotomy, may be indicated.

Cricothyroidotomy. Significant airway obstruction in the combat setting is likely the result of penetrating wounds of the face or neck, where blood or disrupted anatomy precludes good visualization of the vocal cords. This setting makes endotracheal intubation highly difficult, if not impossible. In these cases, surgical cricothyroidotomy is preferable over endotracheal intubation. This procedure has been reported safe and effective in trauma victims, and in the hands of a rescuer who does not intubate on a regular basis, it should be the next step when other airway devices are not effective.

Intubation. Endotracheal intubation is the preferred airway technique in civilian trauma settings, but this procedure may be prohibitively difficult in the tactical environment. Many medics have never intubated a live person; their experience is only with mannequins in a controlled environment and is infrequent at best. The standard endotracheal intubation technique requires the use of tactically compromising white light. Also, esophageal intubations are more likely with the inexperienced intubator and much more difficult to detect in the tactical environment. Finally, most airway obstructions on the battlefield are the result of penetrating wounds of the head and neck, where cricothyroidotomy is the procedure of choice.

Vascular Access

If the casualty requires fluid resuscitation, then sternal intraosseous (IO) access is recommended due to the preservation of the sternum by the body armor and the speed of the procedure. This site offers rapid access for the administration of pain medications or resuscitation fluids as needed. One possible IO fluid delivery system is the First Access for Shock and Trauma (FAST1) System. Other extremity IO devices are available, but it should be remembered that the majority of injuries are penetrating lower extremity injuries. Humeral head IO devices have become popular in medical evacuation platforms and Role 1 resulting in marked success in the rapid administration of blood products.[21]

If a patient requires more than one access point for multiple medications and fluids, and extremity IO devices are not an option, intravenous access may be attempted. While ATLS training teaches to start two large-bore (14- or 16-gauge) intravenous (IV) catheters, the use of a single 18-gauge catheter is preferred in the tactical setting. The 18-gauge catheter is adequate for rapid delivery of resuscitation fluids and medication, is easier to insert than larger-bore catheters, and conserves the supplies in a medic aid bag. Medics should not start an IV or IO on an extremity that may have a significant wound proximal to the insertion site.

Venous cutdowns are not recommended in the tactical setting because they are time-consuming, technically difficult when fine motor skills are being challenged, and require instruments that in all likelihood will not be available. Medics will most likely not be trained, equipped, or authorized to perform the procedure; therefore, prehospital cutdowns should be limited to a Role 1 facility.

Fluid Resuscitation

Fluid resuscitation during the tactical field care phase is significantly different than in the civilian prehospital setting. During this phase of care, fluid resuscitation is guided by several assumptions:

- The tactical situation may not allow time for thorough fluid resuscitation. Care may consist only of immediate evacuation while in extremis.

- Lack of compressible hemorrhage control is the leading cause of potentially survivable death on the battlefield. Therefore, hemorrhage control is paramount and takes priority over fluid resuscitation, especially in a situation with limited time and resources.

- Stethoscopes, blood pressure cuffs, and other equipment used in the hospital setting to monitor fluid status and shock are rarely available or useful in a noisy and chaotic battlefield environment. The presence of a casualty's peripheral pulse is a crude, but effective, means of determining adequate perfusion of vital organs.[22] In the tactical setting, assessing a casualty's mental status and peripheral pulses is adequate for determining the need for fluid resuscitation.

In light of these considerations, during the tactical field care phase, fluid resuscitation should only be provided to those casualties exhibiting signs of shock or traumatic brain injury (TBI).[23] If the casualty has only superficial wounds, IV fluid resuscitation is not necessary, but oral fluids should be encouraged. In those casualties with significant wounds who are coherent and without any obvious blood loss or signs of shock, blood loss likely has been stopped. In these casualties, obtain IO and/or IV access, hold IV fluids, and re-evaluate the casualty's peripheral pulses and mental status as frequently as possible.

Shock. Shock encountered in the combat setting will most likely be hemorrhagic shock. Assume the casualty is in shock if he has an altered mental status in the absence of head injury and/or has weak or absent radial pulses. If the casualty's peripheral pulse is absent or there is a decrease in the level of consciousness in the absence of a head injury, then initiate fluid resuscitation.[24]

- During the tactical field care phase, 6 percent Hetastarch (Hextend) is the recommended fluid for resuscitation. Hextend is preferred over crystalloid fluids because one 500-milliliter (ml) bag of Hextend is physiologically equivalent to three 1,000-ml bags of Lactated Ringer's solution (LR), weighs 5.5 pounds less, and expands intravascular fluid volume for at least 8 hours.

- Initiate fluid resuscitation with a 500-ml Hextend IV bolus.

- Monitor the casualty, and, if after 30 minutes the casualty still has no radial pulse or altered mentation, administer a second 500-ml Hextend bolus.

- Do not administer more than 1,000 ml of Hextend. This is equivalent to 6 liters of LRS.

If the casualty is still in shock after 1,000 ml of Hextend, the casualty is probably still bleeding. Fluid resuscitation is unlikely to be effective until the hemorrhage is controlled. The casualty needs to be evacuated to surgical care as soon as possible. If rapid evacuation is not feasible, the medic may need to consider triaging medical supplies and focusing attention on more salvageable casualties. Role 1 providers should consider implementing the walking blood bank per theater protocol and the Joint Trauma System Clinical Practice Guidelines (CPGs).[25]

TBI. Head injuries are special situations. Hypotension and hypoxia exacerbate secondary brain injury and are difficult to control in the initial phases of combat casualty care. If the casualty with a TBI is unconscious and has no peripheral pulse, then he should be resuscitated to restore a palpable radial pulse and evacuated as soon as possible.

Hypothermia Prevention

Although not included in earlier research, hypothermia is widely accepted as the fourth potentially survivable cause of death on the battlefield. Combat casualties are at a high risk for hypothermia, defined as a whole body temperature below 95 F (35 C). Hypothermia can occur regardless of the ambient temperature. The blood loss typically associated with combat trauma results in peripheral vasoconstriction, which contributes to the development of hypothermia. In addition, the longer a casualty is exposed to the environment during treatment and evacuation, especially in wet conditions, the more likely the development of hypothermia will occur. This is even more the case during rotary-wing evacuation.

Hypothermia, acidosis, and coagulopathy constitute the "lethal triad" in trauma patients. The association of hypothermic coagulopathy with high mortality has been well described. Hypothermia causes the inhibition of coagulation proteins, thus exacerbating the bleeding problem. The need to prevent hypothermia is highlighted by the fact that up to 10 percent of combat casualties arrive at a level III treatment facility exhibiting some degree of hypothermia.

During the tactical field care phase, the rescuer must first minimize the casualty's exposure to the elements. If possible, keep all protective gear on the patient and replace any wet clothing. Use any method available to keep the casualty warm, such as dry blankets, poncho liners, and sleeping bags.

Hypothermia prevention equipment is readily available to all medics. The Ready-Heat blanket actively warms to 110-118 F when opened and serves as the heat source. When the casualty is ready for transport, place the

Ready-Heat blanket onto the casualty's torso, with the tails tucked under the heating elements to protect from burns, and then place the casualty into a warming blanket, such as a Blizzard survival blanket or Heat-Reflective Shell.[26]

Monitoring/Further Evaluation

During the tactical field care phase, monitor the casualty clinically and frequently reassess until evacuation. Pulse oximetry, at a minimum, should be included in the medic aid bag and used as an adjunct to clinical monitoring. Keep in mind that pulse oximetry readings may be misleading in the setting of shock and hypothermia. Care should prevail with the interpretation of pulse oximetry readings at extreme elevations during tactical operations in areas of high altitude.

Carefully check the casualty for additional wounds. High-velocity projectiles from assault rifles may tumble and take erratic courses in tissue, leading to exit sites removed from the entry wound. Inspect and dress all wounds.

Pain Control

All casualties in pain should be given analgesia. The type and route of medication is dependent upon whether the casualty is conscious, still able to fight, and if IO/IV access has been obtained.

Able to fight. If the casualty is conscious and still able to fight, give oral pain medications that will not alter the level of consciousness. The recommended medications are Meloxicam (Mobic), 15 milligrams (mg) once daily, along with two 650-mg bilayered Tylenol caplets; this should be followed by two Tylenol caplets every eight hours.[27] These medications, along with an oral antibiotic, make up the combat pill pack, which all combatants should be instructed to take when they sustain a penetrating wound on the battlefield (see Appendix E).

Unable to fight. If the casualty is seriously injured, in pain, and otherwise unable to fight, he should be given narcotic medications. Medics must be trained in the use of Naloxone (Narcan) and have it readily available before administering any narcotics. Closely monitor the casualty for any respiratory depression. Clearly and visibly document the use of any narcotics to avoid overdose and respiratory compromise. The following medications are options based on unit and theater policy:

- Oral transmucosal fentanyl citrate (OTFC), 800 mg transbuccaly.[28]

    OR

- Ketamine, 50-100 mg IM or 50 mg intranasal.

    OR

- Morphine sulfate, 5 mg morphine sulfate IO/IV.

Fractures

Splint all fractures as circumstances allow, ensuring that peripheral pulse, sensory, and motor checks are performed both before and after splinting. Be aware of possible compartment syndrome with suspected fractures associated with blast-injured Soldiers. The absence of a distal pulse with a possible fracture should be cause for more immediate evacuation.

Pelvic stabilization has become an important aspect in the treatment of combat casualties due to the evolving injury patterns on the modern battlefield. Most pelvic fractures are difficult to diagnose in a prehospital environment and are ultimately diagnosed by radiograph upon arrival at a Role 3 facility. After action reports support the use of circumferential pelvic stabilization in casualties with injuries between the mid-thigh and umbilicus and/or bilateral lower extremity amputations. Optimal reduction of pelvic fractures is obtained through the application of circumferential compression around the greater trochanters.[29] A pelvic sling with integrated tension control aids in preventing the application of too much compression and prevents further injury to the casualty.

Infection Control

Infection is a significant cause of morbidity and mortality in battlefield wounds. Assume all open wounds on the battlefield are infected and treat them with antibiotics. Choose antibiotics that cover a broad spectrum of organisms, with the specific medications based on available delivery route and any medication allergies the casualty may have.

Able to take oral medication. If the casualty can take oral medications, then 400 mg of Moxafloxacin, taken once daily, is recommended. This medication should be part of the combat pill pack. The casualty should take this as soon as he is injured and all life-threatening injuries have been addressed.

Unable to take oral medication. If the casualty is unable to take oral medications because of shock, unconsciousness, or other reasons, then IO, IV, or intramuscular (IM) antibiotics should be given. Recommended antibiotics in this case include Cefazolin, 2 grams (g) IV;[30] or Cefotetan, 2 g IV (over 3 to 5 minutes) or IM every 12 hours; or Ertapenem, 1 g IV (over 30 minutes) or IM every 24 hours.

Penetrating Eye Trauma

Penetrating eye trauma presents a problem with care providers on the battlefield. These injuries can deteriorate without proper care. If a penetrating eye injury is suspected, perform a rapid field test of the individual's visual acuity. It is not necessary to use a vision (Snellen) chart to do so. Have the patient read any printed material or try to determine how many fingers you are holding up, or see if the patient can distinguish between light and dark. If vision is impaired, apply a rigid eye shield over the eye (not a pressure bandage). See Figure 1-3, below. Avoid placing any pressure on the globe of the eye since this could cause the internal contents of the eye to be pushed out. If available, give the casualty a 400-mg Moxifloxacin tablet to provide antibiotic coverage.

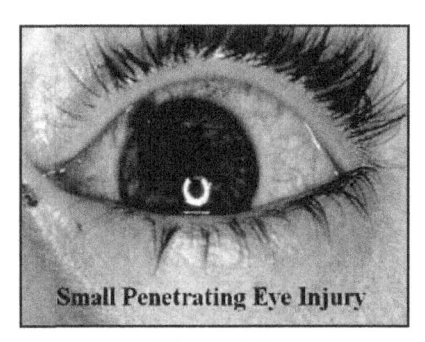

Figure 1-2

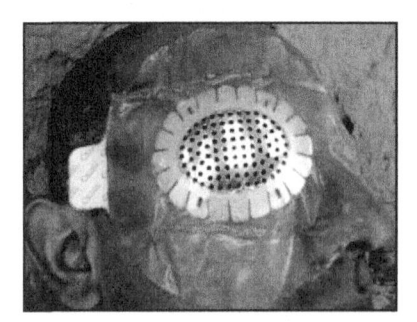

Figure 1-3

Burns

Burn casualties should have their wounds covered with dry, sterile bandages. Avoid using "WaterGel" directly on the burns. Calculate the total body surface area (TBSA) of the burn by using the "Rule of Nines."

Rule of Nines

You can estimate the TBSA that has been burned on an adult by using multiples of 9. The percentage of the body involved can be calculated as follows:

Head = 9%

Chest (front) = 9%

Abdomen (front) = 9%

Upper/mid/low back and buttocks = 18%

Each arm = 9% (front = 4.5%, back = 4.5%)

Groin = 1%

Each leg = 18% total (front = 9%, back = 9%)

Burns to the face and neck should raise the suspicion for airway compromise, and the provider should be prepared to initiate emergency airway support if necessary.

Fluid resuscitation should be accomplished by using the "Rule of Ten." Fluid resuscitation should be provided to casualties with TBSA burns greater than 20 percent.

Rule of Ten

Calculate the TBSA of the burns to the nearest 10 percent.

- Example: 43% TBSA burn would become 40%, 46% TBSA burn would become 50%.

Fluid resuscitation protocol:

Initial IV/IO fluid rate is calculated as % TBSA x 10 cubic centimeters (cc)/hour for adults weighing 40-80 kilograms (kg). For every 10 kg above 80 kg, increase initial rate by 100 ml/hour.

Examples:

- Casualty who weighs 50 kg and has a 40% TBSA burn: 40 x 10 ml = 400 ml per hour. If possible, monitor urine output to 30-50 ml/hour.
- If casualty is 90 kg with a 40% TBSA, the formula would be 40 x 10 mls = 400 ml/hour + 100 ml, for a total of 500 ml/hour.

The fluid of choice for isolated burns is LR. If the casualty has additional wounds and has lost blood, Hextend may be used to prevent or treat shock. The amount of Hextend used should not exceed 1,000 mls, as in the hypovolemic shock protocol.

Analgesia for burns should follow the guidelines in the paragraphs above for significant pain.

Antibiotics are not required for burns alone, but may be appropriate for other penetrating injuries.

The key to successful burn management is to evacuate the casualty to definitive care as rapidly as possible.

Spinal Precautions

Care under fire. Direct the casualty to move to cover and apply self-aid if able. If the casualty requires assistance, move him to cover. If the mechanism of injury included blunt trauma (such as riding in a vehicle that was struck by an improvised explosive device), minimize spinal movement while extricating him from the vehicle and moving him to cover. The casualty should be moved along his long spinal axis if at all possible when attempting to stabilize the head and neck.

Tactical field care, tactical evacuation care. Use spinal motion restriction techniques as defined below for casualties whose mechanism of injury included blunt trauma if: (a) they are unconscious; (b) they are conscious and have midline cervical spine tenderness or midline back pain; or (c) they are conscious but demonstrate neurologic injury, such as inability to move their arms and/or legs, sensory deficits, or paresthesias.

Spinal motion restriction techniques. For these casualties, leave the individual body armor in place to protect the thoracic spine after evaluation and lifesaving interventions are performed. The cervical spine may be protected by using a cervical stabilization device in conjunction with the casualty's individual body armor, or by an additional first responder holding the casualty's head to maintain alignment with the thoracic spine. Spine boards should be used in addition to these measures when available.

Communication

Combat is a frightening experience. Being wounded, especially seriously, can generate tremendous anxiety and fear. Engaging a casualty with reassurance is therapeutically beneficial. Communication is just as important in casualty care on the battlefield as it is in the treatment facility. Ensure the care plan is explained to the casualty.

Documentation

Battlefield documentation of injuries and care rendered in the prehospital arena is sorely lacking. There is a tremendous need for documenting clinical assessments, treatment rendered, and changes in the casualty's status, and also forwarding that information with the casualty to the next level of care. Use Department of the Army (DA) Form 7656, *Tactical Combat Casualty Care Card,* for this purpose (see Figure 1-4). If this form is not available, use 3-inch white tape on the casualty's chest and an indelible pen to document care.

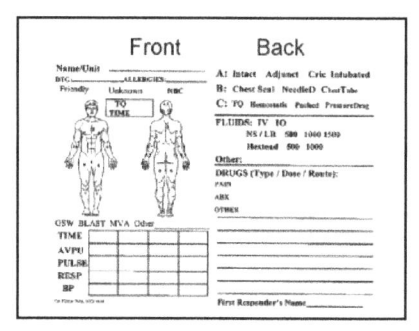

Figure 1-4. DA Form 7656, *Tactical Combat Casualty Care Card*

Note: As of the date of this publication, the TCCC card was under review to be updated and converted to a Department of Defense form.

Section IV: Tactical Evacuation Care

Tactical evacuation care is the care rendered once the casualty has been picked up by an aircraft, vehicle, or boat for transportation to a higher role of care. In general, tactical evacuation care is a continuation of care rendered during the tactical field care phase, with minor additions based on additional medical personnel and equipment accompanying the evacuation asset.

The arrival of additional medical personnel is important for several reasons:

- The medic may be one of the casualties or may be dehydrated, hypothermic, or otherwise debilitated.
- There may be multiple casualties that exceed the medic's capability to provide care simultaneously.

- The evacuation asset's equipment will need to be prepared prior to evacuation.
- Additional medical personnel, such as physicians and other specialists, provide greater expertise.

The additional medical equipment brought by the evacuation asset serves several purposes. Medical resupply may be accomplished during this phase of care. More advanced medical equipment such as blood products and other fluids, electronic monitoring devices, and oxygen may now be used to care for the casualty. This equipment and the possibly improved care environment of the evacuation asset allow more advanced casualty care with more skilled providers during the tactical evacuation phase.

Airway Management

Airway management during the tactical evacuation phase follows the same principles as during the tactical field care phase, with the use of positioning and an NPA as the initial management options. However, the management of an impaired airway is exceedingly difficult during tactical evacuation. It is now appropriate, if the equipment and provider expertise are available, to obtain a more definitive airway if required by the casualty's condition. Possible airway management options include:

Cricothyroidotomy. As in the tactical field care phase, cricothyroidotomy is still an appropriate option when an NPA is not effective. This is still the procedure of choice for penetrating wounds of the face or neck, where blood or disrupted anatomy precludes good visualization of the vocal cords, or in cases of suspected inhalation burns.

Intubation. The conditions of the tactical evacuation phase now make intubation a viable option. If the equipment is available and the care provider has the appropriate expertise, several intubation methods are possible. Supraglottic devices such as the laryngeal mask airway, intubating laryngeal mask airway (ILMA), King Laryngeal Tube (LT), or the combitube are recommended options. These devices provide adequate ventilation without the need for illuminated laryngoscopy; have been used effectively in the prehospital setting; and, in the case of the ILMA, King LT, and combitube, protect the airway from aspiration. Additionally, if personnel have adequate training, endotracheal intubation is now an option.

Breathing

During the tactical evacuation phase, management of the casualty's breathing include a reassessment and continuation of the interventions made during the tactical field care phase. Treat penetrating chest wounds with occlusive dressings and monitor for the development of a tension PTX, which is treated with a needle decompression. At this phase of care, it may now be possible to consider additional interventions.

Chest tubes. For casualties with a tension PTX that fail to show improvement with a needle decompression, the provider should consider inserting a chest tube. A chest tube should also be considered for casualties with PTX when a long evacuation time is anticipated, even if the initial needle decompression was successful.

Oxygen. Oxygen may be brought by the evacuation asset and now be available. Most combat casualties do not require oxygen, but it should be used in seriously injured casualties, especially in the following circumstances:

- Low oxygen saturation by pulse oximetry.
- Injuries associated with impaired oxygenation.
- Unconscious casualties.
- Casualties with TBIs.
- Casualties in shock.
- Casualties at altitude.

Fluid Resuscitation

Several improvements in fluid resuscitation are possible in the tactical evacuation phase. Monitoring equipment brought by the evacuation asset may yield a better understanding of a casualty's fluid status and can direct resuscitation efforts. Continue resuscitation in casualties with a TBI to maintain a systolic blood pressure of at least 90 millimeters (mm) mercury (Hg). If authorized by command policy and they are available, plasma and packed red blood cells in a 1:1 ratio should be given to casualties suffering from blood loss. These blood cells will restore oxygen-carrying capacity.

Hypothermia Prevention

Hypothermia prevention becomes paramount during the tactical evacuation phase, especially if the casualty is evacuated in a helicopter. Continue to follow the hypothermia prevention principles of the tactical field care phase: minimize the casualty's exposure to the elements, replace wet clothing, and use warming equipment as discussed above. If the doors of the evacuation asset must be kept open, protect the casualty from the wind. Also, if portable fluid-warming devices are available, they should be used on all IO/IV fluid sites.

Monitoring

The evacuation asset may contain additional patient-monitoring devices. Electronic systems capable of monitoring blood pressure, heart rate, pulse oximetry, and end-tidal carbon dioxide may be available and should be used. This is especially true in helicopter evacuation, which impairs or prevents the ability to monitor the casualty clinically.

Additional Measures

All other aspects of care during the tactical evacuation phase are identical to those during the tactical field care phase. Hemorrhage must be controlled, using tourniquets as necessary. Maintain vascular access with at least one IO device or an 18-gauge IV, if necessary. Provide analgesia and antibiotics as previously indicated during the tactical field care phase. Continue to document all care, and forward this information with the casualty to the next role of care.

Section V: Management Guidelines

Basic Management Plan for Care Under Fire

1. Return fire and take cover.

2. Direct or expect the casualty to remain engaged as a combatant if appropriate.

3. Direct the casualty to move to cover and apply self-aid if able.

4. Try to keep the casualty from sustaining additional wounds.

5. Casualties should be extricated from burning vehicles or buildings and moved to places of relative safety. Do what is necessary to stop the burning process.

6. Airway management is generally best deferred until the tactical field care phase.

7. Stop life-threatening external hemorrhage if tactically feasible.

- Direct the casualty to control the hemorrhage by self-aid if able.

- Use a tourniquet with windlass for hemorrhage that is anatomically amenable to tourniquet application.

- Apply the tourniquet as high on the bleeding extremity as possible, over the uniform, tighten, and move the casualty to cover.

Basic Management Plan for Tactical Field Care

1. Casualties with an altered mental status should be disarmed immediately.

2. Airway management.

    - Unconscious casualty without airway obstruction:

        o Chin lift or jaw-thrust maneuver.

        o NPA.

        o Place casualty in the recovery position.

    - Casualty with airway obstruction or impending airway obstruction:

        o Chin lift or jaw-thrust maneuver.

        o NPA.

        o Allow casualty to assume any position that best protects the airway, to include sitting up.

        o Place unconscious casualty in the recovery position.

        o If previous measures were unsuccessful, perform surgical cricothyroidotomy (with lidocaine if conscious).

3. Breathing.

    - In a casualty with progressive respiratory distress and known or suspected torso trauma, consider a tension pneumothorax and decompress the chest on the side of the injury with a 14-gauge, 3.25-inch needle/catheter unit inserted in the second intercostal space at the midclavicular line. Ensure the needle entry into the chest is not medial to the nipple line and is not directed toward the heart. An acceptable alternative site is the fourth or fifth intercostals space at the anterior axillary line (AAL).

    - All open and/or sucking chest wounds should be treated by immediately applying an occlusive material to cover the defect and securing it in place. Monitor the casualty for the potential development of a subsequent tension pneumothorax.

    - Casualties with moderate/severe TBI should be given supplemental oxygen when available to maintain oxygen saturation greater than 90 percent.

4. Bleeding.

- Assess for unrecognized hemorrhage and control all sources of bleeding. If not already done, use a tourniquet with windlass to control life-threatening external hemorrhage that is anatomically amenable to tourniquet application or for any traumatic amputation. Apply directly to the skin 2 to 3 inches above the wound.

- For compressible hemorrhage not amenable to tourniquet use or as an adjunct to tourniquet removal (if evacuation time is anticipated to be longer than two hours), use combat gauze as the hemostatic agent of choice. Combat gauze should be applied with at least three minutes of direct pressure. Before releasing any tourniquet on a casualty who has been resuscitated for hemorrhagic shock, ensure a positive response to resuscitation efforts (i.e., a peripheral pulse normal in character and normal mentation if there is no TBI). If a lower extremity wound is not amenable to tourniquet application and cannot be controlled by hemostatics/dressings, consider immediate application of a mechanical junctional hemorrhage control device.

- Reassess prior tourniquet application. Expose wound and determine if tourniquet is needed. If so, move tourniquet from over uniform and apply directly to skin 2 to 3 inches above the wound. If a tourniquet is not needed, use other techniques to control the bleeding.

- When time and the tactical situation permit, a distal pulse check should be accomplished. If a distal pulse is still present, consider additional tightening of the tourniquet or the use of a second tourniquet, side by side and proximal to the first, to eliminate the distal pulse.

- Expose and clearly mark all tourniquet sites with the time of tourniquet application. Use an indelible marker.

5. IV access.

- Start an 18-gauge IV or saline lock if indicated.

- If resuscitation is required and IV access is not obtainable, use the IO route.

6. Tranexamic acid (TXA). If a casualty is anticipated to need significant blood transfusion (for example, presents with hemorrhagic shock, one or more major amputations, penetrating torso trauma, or evidence of severe bleeding):

- Administer 1 g of tranexamic acid in 100 cc normal saline or LRS as soon as possible but NOT later than 3 hours after injury.

- Begin second infusion of 1 g TXA after Hextend or other fluid treatment.

7. Fluid resuscitation. Assess for hemorrhagic shock. Altered mental status (in the absence of head injury) and weak or absent peripheral pulses are the best field indicators of shock.

- If not in shock:
    - No IV fluids are necessary.
    - Per oral (PO) fluids permissible if conscious and able to swallow.
- If in shock:
    - Hextend, 500-ml IV bolus.
    - Repeat once after 30 minutes if still in shock.
    - No more than 1,000 ml of Hextend.

Continued efforts to resuscitate must be weighed against logistical and tactical considerations and the risk of incurring further casualties.

If a casualty with an altered mental status due to a suspected TBI has a weak or absent peripheral pulse, resuscitate as necessary to maintain a palpable radial pulse.

8. Prevention of hypothermia.

- Minimize the casualty's exposure to the elements. Keep protective gear on or with the casualty if feasible.
- Replace wet clothing with dry clothing if possible. Get the casualty onto an insulated surface as soon as possible.
- Apply the Ready-Heat blanket from the hypothermia prevention and management kit (HPMK) to the casualty's torso (not directly on the skin), and cover the casualty with the heat-reflective shell.
- If a heat-reflective shell is not available, the previously recommended combination of the blizzard survival blanket and the Ready-Heat blanket may also be used.
- If the items mentioned above are not available, use dry blankets, poncho liners, sleeping bags, or anything that will retain heat and keep the casualty dry.
- Warm fluids are preferred if IV fluids are required.

TACTICAL COMBAT CASUALTY CARE HANDBOOK

9. Penetrating eye trauma. If a penetrating eye injury is noted or suspected:

    - Perform a rapid field test of visual acuity.
    - Cover the eye with a rigid eye shield (NOT a pressure patch). Ensure that the 400-mg Moxifloxacin tablet in the combat pill pack is taken if possible and IV/IM antibiotics are given as outlined below if oral Moxifloxacin cannot be taken.

10. Monitoring.

    - Pulse oximetry should be available as an adjunct to clinical monitoring. All individuals with moderate/severe TBI should be monitored with pulse oximetry.
    - Readings may be misleading in the settings of shock or marked hypothermia.

11. Inspect and dress known wounds.

12. Check for additional wounds.

13. Provide analgesia as necessary.

Note: Ketamine must not be used if the casualty has suspected penetrating eye injury or significant TBI (evidenced by penetrating brain injury or head injury with altered level of consciousness).

- Able to fight: **Note:** These medications should be carried by the combatant and self-administered as soon as possible after the wound is sustained.
    - Mobic, 15 mg PO once a day.
    - Tylenol, 650-mg bilayer caplet, two PO every 8 hours.
- Unable to fight: (**Note:** Have Naloxone readily available whenever administering opiates.)
- Does not otherwise require IV/IO access.
    - Oral transmucosal fentanyl citrate, 800 mg transbuccally:
        * Recommend taping lozenge-on-a-stick to casualty's finger as an added safety measure.
        * Reassess in 15 minutes.

- * Add second lozenge, in other cheek, as necessary to control severe pain.
- * Monitor for respiratory depression.
- ○ Ketamine 50-100 mg IM.
  - * Repeat dose every 30 minutes to 1 hour as necessary to control severe pain or until the casualty develops nystagmus (rhythmic eye movement back and forth).
- IV or IO access obtained:
  - ○ Morphine sulfate, 5 mg IV/IO:
    - * Reassess in 10 minutes.
    - * Repeat dose every 10 minutes as necessary to control severe pain.
    - * Monitor for respiratory depression.
  - ○ Ketamine, 20 mg slow IV/IO push over 1 minute.
    - * Reassess in 5-10 minutes.
    - * Repeat dose every 5 to 10 minutes as necessary to control severe pain or until the casualty develops nystagmus.
    - * Continue to monitor for respiratory depression and agitation.
  - ○ Promethazine, 25 mg IV/IM/IO:
    - * Every 6 hours as needed for nausea or for synergistic analgesic effect.

Note: Narcotic analgesia should be avoided in casualties with respiratory distress, decreased oxygen saturation, shock, or decreased level of consciousness.

14. Splint fractures and recheck pulse.

15. Antibiotics: Recommended for all open combat wounds.
    - If able to take PO:
      - ○ Moxifloxacin, 400 mg PO, once a day.

- If unable to take PO (shock, unconsciousness):
    - Cefotetan, 2 g IV (slow push over 3 to 5 minutes) or IM every 12 hours.

    OR

    - Ertapenem, 1 g IV/IM once a day.

16. Burns.
    - Facial burns, especially those that occur in closed spaces, may be associated with inhalation injury. Aggressively monitor airway status and oxygen saturation in such patients and consider early surgical airway for respiratory distress or oxygen desaturation.
    - Estimate TBSA burned to the nearest 10 percent using the "Rule of Nines."
    - Cover the burn area with dry, sterile dressings. For extensive burns (greater than 20 percent), consider placing the casualty in the HPMK to both cover the burned areas and prevent hypothermia in accordance with Section III.
    - Fluid resuscitation (U.S. Army Institute of Surgical Research [USAISR] Rule of Ten):
        - If burns are greater than 20 percent of TBSA, fluid resuscitation should be initiated as soon as IV/IO access is established. Resuscitation should be initiated with LRS, normal saline, or Hextend. If Hextend is used, no more than 1,000 ml should be given, followed by LRS or normal saline as needed.
        - Initial IV/IO fluid rate is calculated as % TBSA x 10 cc/hour for adults weighing 40-80 kg.
        - For every 10 kg above 80 kg, increase initial rate by 100 ml/hour.
        - If hemorrhagic shock is also present, resuscitation for hemorrhagic shock takes precedence over resuscitation for burn shock. Administer IV/IO fluids per the TCCC management guidelines.
        - Analgesia in accordance with Section III may be administered to treat burn pain.
        - Prehospital antibiotic therapy is not indicated solely for burns, but antibiotics should be given per the TCCC management guidelines if indicated to prevent infection in penetrating wounds.

- All TCCC interventions can be performed on or through burned skin in a burn casualty.

17. Communicate with the casualty if possible.

- Encourage and reassure the casualty.
- Explain care to the casualty.

18. CPR. Resuscitation on the battlefield for victims of blast or penetrating trauma who have no pulse, no ventilations, and no other signs of life will not be successful and should not be attempted. However, casualties with torso trauma or polytrauma who have no pulse or respirations during tactical field care should have bilateral needle decompression performed to ensure they do not have a tension pneumothorax prior to discontinuation of care. The procedure is the same as described in Section III above.

19. Documentation of care. Document clinical assessments, treatments rendered, and changes in the casualty's status on a TCCC card. Forward this information with the casualty to the next level of care.

Basic Management Plan for Tactical Evacuation Care

The term "tactical evacuation" includes both casualty evacuation and medical evacuation as defined in Joint Publication 4-02, *Doctrine for Health Services Support in Joint Operations.*

1. Airway management.

- Unconscious casualty without airway obstruction:
    - Chin lift or jaw-thrust maneuver.
    - NPA.
    - Place casualty in the recovery position.
- Casualty with airway obstruction or impending airway obstruction:
    - Chin lift or jaw-thrust maneuver.
    - NPA.
    - Allow casualty to assume any position that best protects the airway, to include sitting up.
    - Place unconscious casualty in the recovery position.
    - If above measures are unsuccessful:
        * Supraglottic airway.

- * Endotracheal intubation.
  - * Surgical cricothyroidotomy (with lidocaine if conscious).
- Spinal immobilization is not necessary for casualties with penetrating trauma.

2. Breathing.
   - In a casualty with progressive respiratory distress and known or suspected torso trauma, consider a tension PTX and decompress the chest on the side of the injury with a 14-gauge, 3.25-inch needle/catheter unit inserted in the second intercostal space at the mid-clavicular line. Ensure that the needle entry into the chest is not medial to the nipple line and is not directed toward the heart.
   - Consider chest tube insertion if no improvement and/or long transport is anticipated.
   - Most combat casualties do not require supplemental oxygen, but administration of oxygen may be of benefit for the following types of casualties:
     - Low oxygen saturation by pulse oximetry.
     - Injuries associated with impaired oxygenation.
     - Unconscious casualty.
     - Casualty with TBI (maintain oxygen saturation greater than 90 percent).
     - Casualty in shock.
     - Casualty at altitude.
   - All open and/or sucking chest wounds should be treated by immediately applying an occlusive material to cover the defect and securing it in place. Monitor the casualty for the potential development of a subsequent tension PTX.

3. Bleeding.
   - Assess for unrecognized hemorrhage and control all sources of bleeding. If not already done, use a Committee on Tactical Combat Casualty Care (CoTCCC)-recommended tourniquet to control life-threatening external hemorrhage that is anatomically amenable to tourniquet application or for any traumatic amputation. Apply directly to the skin 2 to 3 inches above the wound.

- For compressible hemorrhage not amenable to tourniquet use or as an adjunct to tourniquet removal (if evacuation time is anticipated to be longer than two hours), use combat gauze as the hemostatic agent of choice. Combat gauze should be applied with at least three minutes of direct pressure. Before releasing any tourniquet on a casualty who has been resuscitated for hemorrhagic shock, ensure there is a positive response to resuscitation efforts (i.e., a peripheral pulse normal in character and normal mentation if there is no TBI.) If a lower extremity wound is not amenable to tourniquet application and cannot be controlled by hemostatics/dressings, consider immediate application of mechanical direct pressure, including CoTCCC-recommended devices such as the combat ready clamp.

- Reassess prior tourniquet application. Expose the wound and determine if a tourniquet is needed. If so, move the tourniquet from over the uniform and apply directly to the skin 2 to 3 inches above the wound. If a tourniquet is not needed, use other techniques to control the bleeding.

- When time and the tactical situation permit, a distal pulse check should be accomplished. If a distal pulse is still present, consider additional tightening of the tourniquet or the use of a second tourniquet, side by side and proximal to the first, to eliminate the distal pulse.

- Expose and clearly mark all tourniquet sites with the time of tourniquet application. Use an indelible marker.

4. IV access. Reassess need for IV access:

- If indicated, start an 18-gauge IV or saline lock.
- If resuscitation is required and IV access is not obtainable, use IO route.

5. TXA. If a casualty is anticipated to need a significant blood transfusion (for example, presents with hemorrhagic shock, one or more major amputations, penetrating torso trauma, or evidence of severe bleeding):

- Administer 1 g of tranexamic acid in 100 cc normal saline or Lactated Ringers as soon as possible but NOT later than 3 hours after injury.
- Begin second infusion of 1 gm TXA after Hextend or other fluid treatment.

6. TBI.

- Casualties with moderate/severe TBI should be monitored for:
    - Decrease in level of consciousness.

- Pupillary dilation.
- Systolic blood pressure should be greater than 90 mm Hg.
- Oxygen saturation greater than 90 percent.
- Hypothermia.
- Partial pressure of carbon dioxide (PCO2) (if capnography is available, maintain between 35-40 mm Hg).
- Penetrating head trauma (if present, administer antibiotics).
- Assume a spinal (neck) injury until cleared.

- Unilateral papillary dilation accompanied by a decreased level of consciousness may signify impending cerebral herniation. If these signs occur, take the following action to decrease intracranial pressure:
  - Administer 250 cc of a 3-percent or 5-percent hypertonic saline bolus.
  - Elevate the casualty's head 30 degrees.
  - Hyperventilate the casualty.
    * Respiratory rate of 20 per minute.
    * Capnography should be used to maintain an end tidal carbon dioxide (CO2) between 30-35.
    * The highest oxygen concentration (FIO2) possible should be used for hyperventilation.

Notes:

Do not hyperventilate unless signs of impending herniation are present.

Casualties may hyperventilated with oxygen using the bag valve mask technique.

7. Fluid resuscitation. Reassess for hemorrhagic shock (altered mental status in the absence of brain injury and/or change in pulse character). If blood pressure monitoring is available, maintain target systolic blood pressure 80-90 mm Hg.

- If not in shock:
  - No IV fluids necessary.
  - PO fluids permissible if casualty is conscious and can swallow.

- If in shock and blood products are not available:
    - Hextend, 500-ml IV bolus.
        * Repeat after 30 minutes if still in shock.
        * Continue resuscitation with Hextend or crystalloid solution as needed to maintain target blood pressure or clinical improvement.
- If in shock and blood products are available under an approved command or theater protocol:
    - Resuscitate with two units of plasma followed by packed red blood cells in a 1:1 ratio. If blood component therapy is not available, transfuse fresh whole blood. Continue resuscitation as needed to maintain target blood pressure or clinical improvement.
- If a casualty with an altered mental status due to a suspected TBI has a weak or absent peripheral pulse, resuscitate as necessary to maintain a palpable radial pulse. If blood pressure monitoring is available, maintain target systolic blood pressure of at least 90 mm Hg.

8. Prevention of hypothermia.
    - Minimize the casualty's exposure to the elements. Keep protective gear on or with the casualty if feasible.
    - Replace wet clothing with dry if possible. Get the casualty onto an insulated surface as soon as possible.
    - Apply the Ready-Heat blanket to the casualty's torso (not directly on the skin), and cover the casualty with the Blizzard Blanket or heat-reflective shell.
    - If the items mentioned above are not available, use poncho liners, sleeping bags, or anything that will retain heat and keep the casualty dry.
    - Use a portable fluid warmer capable of warming all IV/IO fluids, including blood products.
    - Protect the casualty from the wind if the doors to the evacuation asset must be kept open.

9. Penetrating eye trauma. If a penetrating eye injury is noted or suspected:
    - Perform a rapid field test of visual acuity.
    - Cover the eye with a rigid eye shield (NOT a pressure patch).

- Ensure the 400-mg Moxifloxacin tablet in the combat pill pack is taken if possible and that IV/IO/IM antibiotics are given as outlined below if oral Moxifloxacin cannot be taken.

10. Monitoring.
    - Institute pulse oximetry and other electronic monitoring of vital signs, if indicated.
    - All individuals with moderate/severe TBI should be monitored with pulse oximetry.
11. Inspect and dress known wounds if not already done.
12. Check for additional wounds.
13. Provide analgesia as necessary.

Note: Ketamine must not be used if the casualty has suspected penetrating eye injury or significant TBI (evidenced by penetrating brain injury or head injury with altered level of consciousness).

- Able to fight: **Note:** These medications should be carried by the combatant and self-administered as soon as possible after the wound is sustained.
    - Mobic, 15 mg PO once a day.
    - Tylenol, 650-mg bilayer caplet, two PO every 8 hours.
- Unable to fight: **Note:** Have Naloxone readily available whenever administering opiates.
- Does not otherwise require IV/IO access:
    - Oral transmucosal fentanyl citrate (OTFC), 800 mg transbuccally:
        * Recommend taping lozenge-on-a-stick to casualty's finger as an added safety measure.
        * Reassess in 15 minutes.
        * Add second lozenge, in other cheek, as necessary to control severe pain.
        * Monitor for respiratory depression.

  OR

    - Ketamine 50-100 mg IM.

- - - * Repeat dose every 30 minutes to 1 hour as necessary to control severe pain or until the casualty develops nystagmus (rhythmic eye movement back and forth).
  - Ketamine 50 mg intranasal (using nasal atomizer device).
    * Repeat dose every 30 minutes to 1 hour as necessary to control severe pain or until the casualty develops nystagmus.
- IV or IO access obtained:
  - Morphine sulfate, 5 mg IV/IO.
    * Reassess in 10 minutes.
    * Repeat dose every 10 minutes as necessary to control severe pain.
    * Monitor for respiratory depression.

      OR

  - Ketamine, 20 mg slow IV/IO push over 1 minute.
    * Reassess in 5-10 minutes.
    * Repeat dose every 5-10 minutes as necessary to control severe pain or until the casualty develops nystagmus.
    * Continue to monitor for respiratory depression and agitation.
  - Promethazine, 25 mg IV/IM/IO:
    * Repeat every 6 hours as needed for nausea or for synergistic analgesic effect.

Note: Narcotic analgesia should be avoided in casualties with respiratory distress, decreased oxygen saturation, shock, or decreased level consciousness.

14. Reassess fractures and recheck pulses.

15. Antibiotics: Recommended for all open combat wounds.
    - If unable to take PO (shock, unconsciousness):
      - Cefotetan, 2 g IV (slow push over 3 to 5 minutes) or IM every 12 hours.

        OR

      - Ertapenem, 1 g IV/IM once a day.

TACTICAL COMBAT CASUALTY CARE HANDBOOK

16. Burns.

- Facial burns, especially those that occur in closed spaces, may be associated with inhalation injury. Aggressively monitor airway status and oxygen saturation in such patients and consider early surgical airway for respiratory distress or oxygen desaturation.

- Estimate TBSA burned to the nearest 10 percent using the Rule of Nines.

- Cover the burn area with dry, sterile dressings. For extensive burns (greater than 20 percent), consider placing the casualty in the Blizzard Blanket and Ready-Heat to both cover the burned areas and prevent hypothermia in accordance with tactical field care above.

- Fluid resuscitation (USAISR Rule of Ten):

    o If burns are greater than 20 percent of the TBSA, fluid resuscitation should be initiated as soon as IV/IO access is established. Resuscitation should be initiated with LRS, normal saline, or Hextend. If Hextend is used, no more than 1,000 ml should be given, followed by Lactated Ringers or normal saline as needed.

    o Initial IV/IO fluid rate is calculated as % TBSA x 10 cc/hour for adults weighing 40-80 kg.

    o For every 10 kg above 80 kg, increase initial rate by 100 ml/hour.

    o If hemorrhagic shock is also present, resuscitation for hemorrhagic shock takes precedence over resuscitation for burn shock. Administer IV/IO fluids per the TCCC guidelines.

- Analgesia in accordance as described above may be administered to treat burn pain.

- Prehospital antibiotic therapy is not indicated solely for burns, but antibiotics should be given per the TCCC guidelines if indicated to prevent infection in penetrating wounds.

- All TCCC interventions can be performed on or through burned skin in a burn casualty.

17. The Pneumatic Antishock Garment (PASG) may be useful for stabilizing pelvic fractures and controlling pelvic and abdominal bleeding. Application and extended use must be carefully monitored. The PASG is contraindicated for casualties with thoracic or brain injuries.

18. CPR in tactical evacuation care.

- Casualties with torso trauma or polytrauma who have no pulse or respirations during tactical evacuation care should have bilateral needle decompression performed to ensure they do not have a tension PTX. The procedure is the same as described in tactical field care above.
- CPR may be attempted during this phase of care if the casualty does not have obviously fatal wounds and will be arriving at a facility with a surgical capability within a short period of time. CPR should not be done at the expense of compromising the mission or denying lifesaving care to other casualties.

19. Documentation of care. Document clinical assessments, treatments rendered, and changes in casualty's status on a TCCC card. Forward this information with the casualty to the next level of care.

Endnotes

1. Bellamy, R.F. "The Causes of Death in Conventional Land Warfare: Implications for Combat Casualty Care Research." *Military Medicine*. 149:55, 1984.

2. Bellamy, R.F. "The Causes of Death in Conventional Land Warfare: Implications for Combat Casualty Care Research." *Military Medicine*. 149:55, 1984.

3. Butler, F.K. Jr., J. Hagmann, and E.G. Butler. "Tactical Combat Casualty Care in Special Operations." *Military Medicine*.161, Suppl.: 3–16, 1996.

4. Butler, F.K. "Tactical Combat Casualty Care: Combining Good Medicine with Good Tactics." *Journal of Trauma*. 54: 2003.

5. Bellamy, R.F. "The Causes of Death in Conventional Land Warfare: Implications for Combat Casualty Care Research." *Military Medicine*. 149:55, 1984.

6. Eastridge, B.J., R.L. Mabry, P. Seguin, et al. "Death on the Battlefield (2001-2011): Implications for the Future of Combat Casualty Care." *Journal of Trauma*. 73(6) Suppl.: 5. 2012.

7. Kragh, J.F., M.L. O'Neill, T.J. Walters, et al. "The Military Emergency Tourniquet Program's Lessons Learned with Devices and Designs." *Military Medicine*. 176:10, 1144, 2011; Kragh, J.F., T.J. Walters, D.G. Baer, et al. "Survival with Emergency Tourniquet Use to Stop Bleeding in Major Limb Trauma." *Annals of Surgery*. 249 (1): 1–7, 2009; Kragh, J.F., M.L. Littrel, J.A. Jones, et al. "Battle Casualty Survival with Emergency Tourniquet Use to Stop Limb Bleeding." *Journal of Emergency Medicine*. 41(6): 590-597.

8. Mott, J.C. *Prehospital Trauma Life Support Manual: Tactical Emergency Medical Support, 8th ed.* Ch. 23. Jones and Bartlett. In Press.

9. McKay, S., D. Callaway. *Rounding out the Warrior, Part II: Assault Rescue: Point of Wounding Extraction.* National Officers Tactical Association.

10. Arishita, G.I., J.S. Vayer, and R.F. Bellamy. "Cervical Spine Immobilization of Penetrating Neck Wounds in a Hostile Environment." *Journal of Trauma*. 1989, 29: 1453–1454.

11. DuBose, J., G.R. Teixeira, P. Hadjizacharia, et al. "The Role of Routine Spinal and Immobilization in Asymptomatic Patients after Gunshot Wounds." *Injury*. 40(8), 860-863. 2009; Stuke, L.E., P.T. Pons, J.S. Guy, et al. "Prehospital Spine Immobilization for Penetrating Trauma: Review and Recommendations from the Prehospital Trauma Life Support Executive Committee." *Journal of Trauma*.71(3), 2011.

12. Rosemary, A.S., P.A. Norris, S.M. Olson, et al. "Prehospital Traumatic Cardiac Arrest: The Cost of Futility." *Journal of Trauma*. 38: 468–474, 1998; Stockinger, Z.T. and N.E. McSwain. "Additional Evidence in Support of Withholding or Terminating Cardiopulmonary Resuscitation for Trauma Patients in the Field." *Journal of the American College of Surgeons*. 198(2), 227-231. 2004.

13. Mott, J.C. *Prehospital Trauma Life Support Manual: Tactical Emergency Medical Support, 8th ed.* Ch. 23. Jones and Bartlett. In Press.

14. Dubick, M.A. and J.F. Kragh. "Evaluation of the Combat Ready Clamp to Control Bleeding in Human Cadavers, Manikins, Swine Femoral Artery Hemorrhage Model and Swine Carcasses." U.S. Army Institutional Report. June 2012.

15. Mott, J.C. *Prehospital Trauma Life Support Manual: Tactical Emergency Medical Support, 8th ed.* Ch. 23. Jones and Bartlett. In Press.

16. Kragh, J.F., M.L. O'Neill, T.J. Walters, et al. "The Military Emergency Tourniquet Program's Lessons Learned with Devices and Designs." *Military Medicine*. 176:10, 1144, 2011.

17. Kragh, J.F., M.L. Littrel, J.A. Jones, et al. "Battle Casualty Survival with Emergency Tourniquet Use to Stop Limb Bleeding." *Journal of Emergency Medicine*. 41(6): 590-597.

18. Otten, M. "Management of Open Sucking Chest Wounds." Committee on Tactical Combat Casualty Care (TCCC) meeting proposed Tactical Combat Casualty Care Guideline Change. 24 July 2008.

19. Harcke, H.T., L.A. Pearse, A.D. Levy, J.M. Getz, and S.R. Robinson. "Chest Wall Thickness in Military Personnel: Implications for Needle Thoracentesis in Tension Pneumothorax." *Military Medicine*. 172: 1260-1263. 2007; Butler, F. "Tactical Combat Casualty Care: Update 2009." *Journal of Trauma*. 691(1). S10-S13. 2010.

20. Inaba, K., B.C. Branco, M. Eckstein, et al. "Optimal Positioning for Emergent Needle Thoracostomy: A Cadaver-based Study. *Journal of Trauma*. 71(5). 1099-1103. 2011.

21. Rush, S. "Cadaver Lab Training for Humeral Head IO Insertion." Military Health System Research Symposium. August 2013.

22. McManus, J., A.L. Yerhov, and D. Ludwig. "Radial Pulse Character Relationships to Systolic Blood Pressure and Trauma Outcomes." *Prehospital Emergency Care*. 9(4). 423-428.

23. Morrison, C.A., M.M. Carrick, M.A. Norman, et al. "Hypotensive Resuscitation Strategy Reduces Transfusion Requirements and Severe Postoperative Coagulopathy in Trauma Patients with Hemorrhagic Shock: Preliminary Results of a Randomized Controlled Trial." *Journal of Trauma*. 70(3): 652-663, 2011.

24. Butler, F. "Fluid Resuscitation in Tactical Combat Casualty Care: Brief History and Current Status." *Journal of Trauma*. 70(5).2011.

25. U.S. Army Institute of Surgical Research. *Joint Theater Trauma System Clinical Practice Guidelines: Fresh Whole Blood Transfusion*. October 2012.

26. Allen, P.B., S.W. Salyer, M.A. Dubick, et al. "Preventing Hypothermia: Comparison of Current Devices Used by the U.S. Army in an In Vitro Warmed Fluid Model." *Journal of Trauma*. 69(1): S154-S161, 2010; McKeague, A.L. "Evaluation of Patient Active Warming Systems." Military Health System Research Symposium, Tactical Combat Casualty Care breakout session. Ft. Lauderdale, FL. August 2012.

27. Butler, F. "Fluid Resuscitation in Tactical Combat Casualty Care: Brief History and Current Status." *Journal of Trauma*. 70(5).2011.

28. Kotwal, R., K. O'Connor, J. Holcomb, et al. "A Novel Pain Management Strategy for Combat Casualty Care." *Annals of Emergency Medicine*. 44: 121-127.2004.

29. Bottlang, M., J.C. Krieg, M. Mohr, et al. "Emergent Management of Pelvic Ring Fractures with use of Circumferential Compression." *Journal of Bone and Joint Surgery*. 84(A) Suppl. 2002.

30. Hospenthal, D.R., C.K. Murray, R.C. Anderson, et al. "Guidelines for the Prevention of Infections Associated with Combat-Related Injuries: 2011 Update." *Journal of Trauma*. 71(2) Suppl. 2011.

Chapter 2
Tactical Combat Casualty Care Procedures
Section I: Hemorrhage Control
(Addressed during Care Under Fire and Tactical Field Care Phases)

Combat Application Tourniquet (CAT)

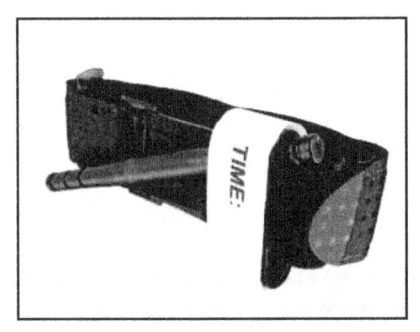

Figure 2-1. Combat Application Tourniquet (CAT)

Figure 2-2

1. During the care under fire phase, place the tourniquet as high on the extremity as possible and over the uniform. (This will be transitioned to a deliberate tourniquet on the skin and 2 inches above the injury in the tactical field care phase.)

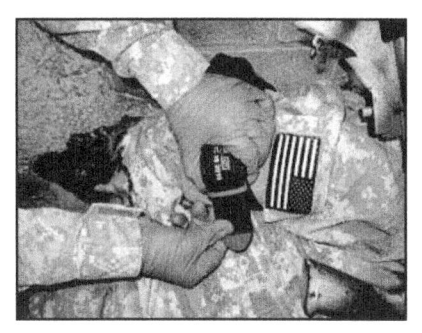

Figure 2-3

2. Route the self-adhering band through the inside slit of the friction adapter buckle. Pull the band tight, removing all slack.

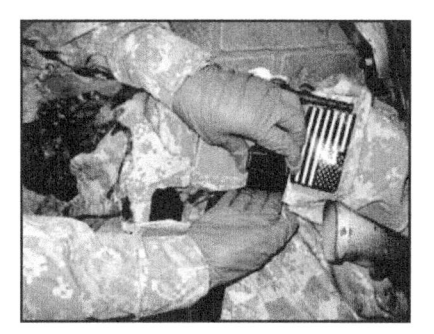

Figure 2-4

3. Feed the self-adhering band tight around the extremity and securely fasten it back on itself. No more than three fingers should fit between the band and the injured extremity.

Note: During self-application of the CAT to an upper extremity wound, defer routing the self-adhering band through both sides of the friction-adapter buckle.

Figure 2-5

4. Twist the windlass rod until the bleeding stops and the distal pulse has been eliminated.

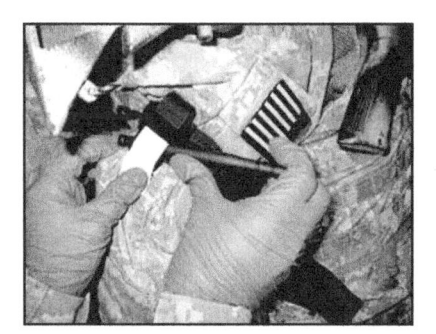

Figure 2-6

5. Lock the windlass rod in place with the windlass clip.

CENTER FOR ARMY LESSONS LEARNED

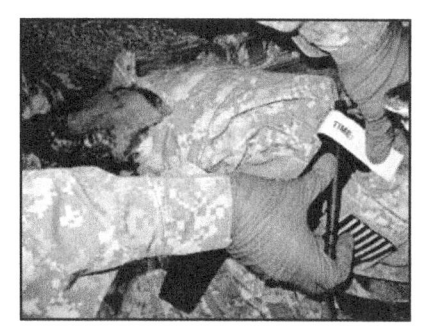

Figure 2-7

6. Grasp the windlass strap, pull tight, and adhere it to the windlass clip.

7. If the tactical situation permits, check for a distal pulse. If a distal pulse is still present, apply a second tourniquet side by side and proximal to the first. Tighten this tourniquet and recheck the distal pulse.

Special Operations Forces Tactical Tourniquet (SOFTT)

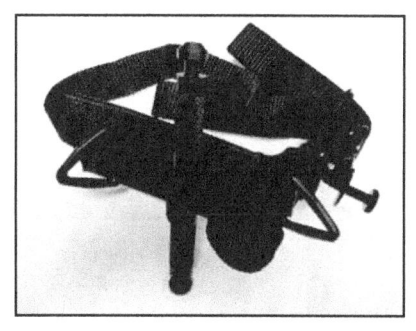

Figure 2-8. Special Operations Forces Tactical Tourniquet (SOFTT)

TACTICAL COMBAT CASUALTY CARE HANDBOOK

Figure 2-9

1. Place the tourniquet as high on the extremity as possible and over the uniform. (This will be transitioned to a deliberate tourniquet on the skin and 2 inches above the injury in the tactical care phase.)

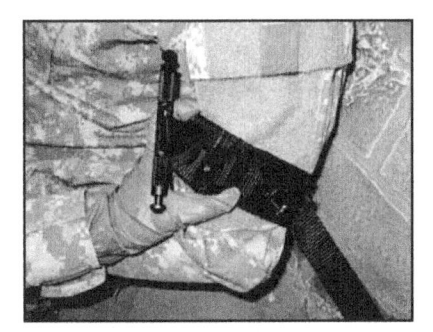

Figure 2-10

2. Pull the tail tight, ensuring to remove as much slack as possible.

Figure 2-11

3. Twist the windlass rod until the bleeding stops.

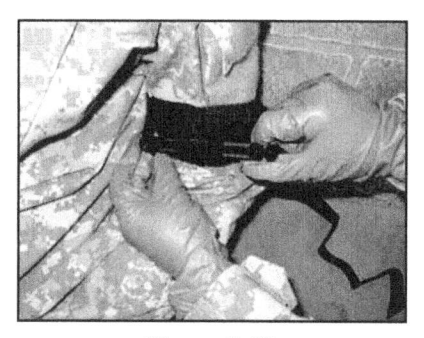

Figure 2-12

4. Lock the windlass rod in place with the windlass tri-ring anchor. It is not necessary to lock both ends of the windlass.

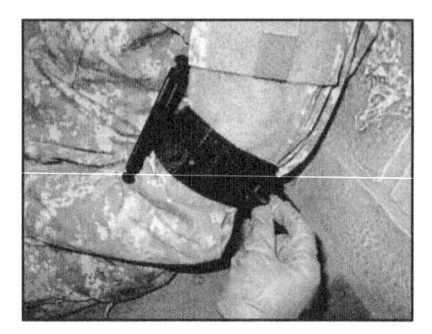

Figure 2-13

5. Twist the set screw clockwise to lock clamp in place.

Combat Gauze

1. Apply dressing with pressure to the wound for 3 minutes.

2. If bleeding continues after 3 minutes of pressure, remove first combat gauze and repeat step 1.

3. Once bleeding is controlled, apply outer bandage (Ace wrap or emergency dressing) to secure the dressing to the wound.

Section II: Airway Management (Addressed during Tactical Field Care and Tactical Evacuation Care Phases)

Nasopharyngeal Airway (NPA) Insertion

1. Place the casualty supine with the head in a neutral position.

> **Caution**: Do not use the NPA if there is clear fluid (cerebrospinal fluid) coming from the ears or nose. This may indicate a skull fracture.

2. Select the appropriately sized airway using one of the following methods:

- Measure the airway from the casualty's nostril to the earlobe.
- Measure the airway from the casualty's nostril to the angle of the jaw.

Note: Choosing the proper length ensures appropriate diameter. Standard adult sizes are 34, 32, 30, and 28 French (Fr).

3. Lubricate the tube with a water-based lubricant.

> **Caution**: Do not use a petroleum-based or non-water-based lubricant. These substances can cause damage to the tissues lining the nasal cavity and pharynx, increasing the risk for infection.

4. Insert the NPA.

- Push the tip of the nose upward gently.
- Position the tube so the bevel of the airway faces toward the septum.
- Insert the airway into the nostril and advance it until the flange rests against the nostril.

> **Caution**: Never force the NPA into the casualty's nostril. If resistance is met, pull the tube out and attempt to insert it in the other nostril. Most attempts to insert the NPA should be in the right nostril. If unable to insert into the right nostril, try the left. If inserting in the left nostril, the bevel will not be against the septum.

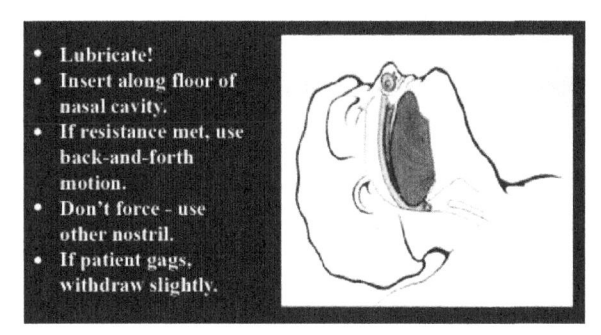

Figure 2-14. Nasopharyngeal Airway (NPA) insertion

Surgical Cricothyroidotomy

Necessary equipment: Prefabricated cricothyroidotomy kit. In the event kits are unavailable, an improvised kit should include a cutting instrument (for example, scalpel no. 10 or no. 15); forceps or tracheal hook; povidone-iodine; endotracheal tube (ETT), 6 millimeter (mm); gloves; 4- x 4-inch gauze; tape; local anesthetic; and materials to inject.

Note: Cricothyroidotomy sets should be prepared prior to the mission. All essential pieces of equipment should be prepared before deployment and packed into a Ziploc bag. Cut the ETT to just above the cuff inflation tube so that the ETT is not protruding 6 inches out of the casualty's neck.

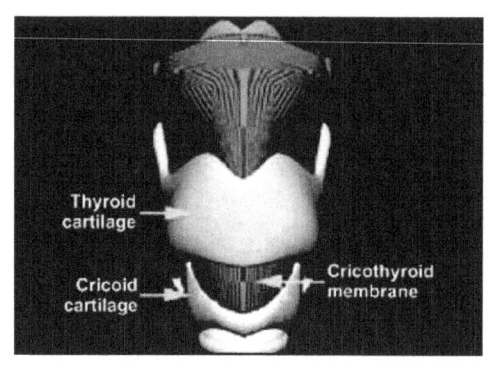

Figure 2-15. Surgical airway (cricothyroidotomy)

1. Hyperextend the casualty's neck.

   - Place the casualty in the supine position.
   - Place a blanket or poncho rolled up under the casualty's neck or between the shoulder blades so that the airway is straight.

Warning: Do not hyperextend the casualty's neck if a cervical injury is suspected.

2. Put on medical gloves, available in the patient's individual first aid kit.

3. Locate the cricothyroid membrane.

   - Place a finger of the nondominant hand on the thyroid cartilage (Adam's apple), and slide the finger down to the cricoid cartilage.
   - Palpate for the "V" notch of the thyroid cartilage.
   - Slide the index finger down into the depression between the thyroid and cricoid cartilage.

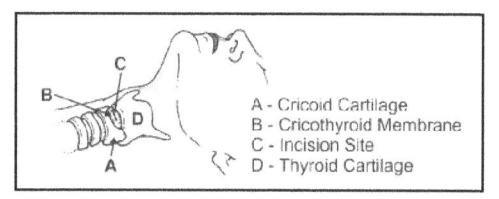

Figure 2-16. Cricothyroid membrane anatomy

4. Prepare the incision site.

- Administer local anesthesia to the incision site if the casualty is conscious.
- Prepare the skin over the membrane with an alcohol pad or povidone-iodine.

5. With a cutting instrument in the dominant hand, make a 1.5-inch vertical incision through the skin over the cricothyroid membrane.

Caution: Do not cut the cricothyroid membrane with this incision.

6. Relocate the cricothyroid membrane by touch and sight.

7. Stabilize the larynx with one hand, and make a 1/2-inch transverse incision through the elastic tissue of the cricothyroid membrane.

Note: A rush of air may be felt through the opening.

8. Dilate the opening with a hemostat or scalpel handle. Hook the cricothyroid membrane with a prefabricated cricothyroid hook or bent 18-gauge needle.

9. Grasp and stabilize the cricoid cartilage.

10. Insert the ETT through the opening and toward the lungs. Only advance the ETT 2 to 3 inches into the trachea to prevent right main stem bronchus intubation. Inflate the cuff to prevent aspiration.

11. Secure the tube circumferentially around the patient's neck to prevent accidental extubation. This can be achieved with tape, tubing, or a prefabricated device in some kits.

12. Check for air exchange and tube placement.

- Air exchange: Listen and feel for air passage through the tube; look for fogging in the tube.

- Tube placement: Bilateral chest sounds/rise and fall of the chest confirm proper tube placement.
- Unilateral breath sounds/rise and fall of chest indicate a right main stem bronchus intubation. Withdraw the ETT 1 to 2 inches and reconfirm placement.
- Air from the casualty's mouth indicates the tube is directed toward the mouth. Remove the tube, reinsert, and recheck for air exchange and placement.
- Any other problem indicates the tube is not placed correctly. Remove the tube, reinsert, and recheck for air exchange.

13. Once the tube is correctly placed, begin rescue breathing, if necessary and tactically appropriate.

- Connect the tube to a bag valve mask and ventilate the casualty at the rate of 20 breaths per minute.
- If a bag valve mask is not available, begin mouth-to-tube resuscitation at 20 breaths per minute.

14. If the patient is breathing spontaneously, ensure the tube is not obstructed and continually assess the need for assisted breathing.

15. Apply a sterile dressing. Use either of the following methods:

- Make a V-shaped fold in a 4- x 4-inch gauze pad and place it under the edge of the ETT to prevent irritation to the casualty. Tape securely.
- Cut two 4- x 4-inch gauze pads half way through and place on opposite sides of the tube. Tape securely.

King Laryngeal Tube (LT) Insertion

(Necessary equipment: King LT, water-based lubricant, and a syringe.)

1. Prepare the casualty.

   - Place the casualty's head in the "sniffing" position.
   - Preoxygenate the casualty, if equipment is available.

2. Prepare the King LT.

   - Choose the appropriately sized tube.

- Test cuff inflation by injecting the proper volume of air into the cuff. Deflate the cuff prior to inserting the tube.
- Lubricate the tube with a water-based lubricant.

> **Caution**: Do not use a petroleum-based or non-water-based lubricant. These substances can cause damage to the tissues lining the nasal cavity and pharynx, increasing the risk for infection.

3. Insert the King LT.
   - Hold the tube in the dominant hand. With the nondominant hand, open the casualty's mouth and apply a chin lift.
   - With the King LT rotated laterally 45 to 90 degrees, place the tip into the mouth and advance the tube behind the base of the tongue.

Note: A lateral approach with the chin lift facilitates proper insertion. The tip must remain midline as it enters the posterior pharynx.

   - Rotate the tube to midline as the tip reaches the posterior pharynx.
   - Advance the tube until the base of the connector is aligned with the teeth or gums.
   - Using either an attached pressure gauge or syringe, inflate the cuff to the minimum volume necessary to seal the airway.

4. Confirm proper placement of the tube.
   - Reference marks for the tube are at the proximal end of the tube and should be aligned with the upper teeth.
   - Confirm proper placement by listening for equal breath sounds during ventilation.
   - While gently ventilating the casualty, withdraw the tube until ventilation is easy and free flowing, with minimal airway pressure needed.

Note: Initially placing the tube deeper than required and then withdrawing slightly increases the chance of proper insertion, helps ensure a patient airway, and decreases the risk of airway obstruction if the casualty spontaneously ventilates.

5. Secure the tube with tape.

Section III: Breathing Management (Addressed during Tactical Field Care and Tactical Evacuation Care Phases)

Penetrating Chest Wounds

Necessary equipment: Prefabricated chest seal or any airtight material (plastic wrap).

1. Expose the wound(s).

   - Cut or unfasten the clothing that covers the wound and expose the casualty's torso from the umbilicus to the Adam's apple circumferentially.
   - Wipe blood/sweat from skin surrounding wound to increase the occlusive seal's effectiveness.
   - Disrupt the wound as little as possible.
   - Apply an occlusive seal to any penetrating injuries on the torso.

Note: Do not remove clothing stuck to the wound.

2. Check for an exit wound.

   - Logroll the casualty and look at the back.
   - Remove the casualty's clothing, if necessary.

3. Seal the wound(s), treating each wound as you go. When not using a prefabricated chest seal, cut the dressing's plastic wrapper on one long and two short sides and remove the dressing.

   - Apply the inner surface of the wrapper to the wound when the casualty exhales.
   - Ensure that the covering extends at least 2 inches beyond the edges of the wound.
   - Seal by applying overlapping strips of tape to all edges of occlusive dressing, forming a complete seal.
   - Cover all wounds in the same manner, as applicable.

Note: All penetrating chest wounds should be treated as if they are penetrating chest wounds.

Note: In an emergency, any airtight material can be used. The material must be large and durable enough so it is not sucked into the chest cavity.

4. Place the casualty on the injured side or sitting up.

5. Monitor the casualty for increasing respiratory difficulty.

- Monitor breathing and the wound seal for continued effectiveness.
- Check vital signs.
- Observe for signs of shock.

Needle Chest Decompression

Necessary equipment: Large-bore needle with catheter (10- to 14-gauge), at least 3.25 inches in length, and tape.

1. Locate the second intercostal space (between the second and third ribs) at the midclavicular line (approximately in line with the nipple) on the affected side of the casualty's chest. An acceptable alternative site used for a chest tube, located at the fourth or fifth rib space at the anterior axillary line (Refer to Figure 2-18).

2. Insert a large-bore (10- to 14-gauge) needle/catheter unit.

- Place the needle tip on the insertion site (between the second and third intercostal space, midclavicular line).
- Lower the proximal end of the needle to permit the tip to enter the skin just above the third rib margin.
- Firmly insert the needle into the skin over the third rib at a 90-degree angle to the chest wall until the pleura has been penetrated, as evidenced by feeling a "pop" as the needle enters the pleural space and a hiss of air escapes from the chest.

Warning: Proper positioning of the needle is essential to avoid puncturing blood vessels and/or nerves. The needle should not be inserted medial to the nipple line, as this will increase the risk of the needle entering the cardiac box.

Note: If you are using a catheter-over-needle, the catheter should be inserted to the hub. Withdraw the needle along the angle of insertion while holding the catheter still.

3. Secure the catheter to the chest with tape and monitor the casualty for possible return of symptoms.

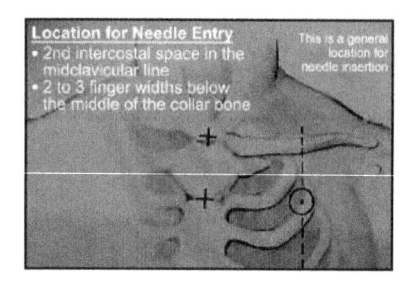

Figure 2-17. Needle chest compression, needle insertion site

Chest Tube Insertion

Necessary equipment: Chest tube (16-35 Fr), gloves, one-way valve, scalpel handle with blades (no. 10 or no. 15), Kelly forceps, large hemostat, povidone-iodine, suture material, lidocaine with 1 percent epinephrine for injection, needle, and syringe.

1. Assess the casualty.

- If necessary, open the airway.

- Ensure adequate respiration and assist as necessary.

- Provide supplemental oxygen, if available.

- Connect the casualty to a pulse oximeter, if available.

2. Prepare the casualty.

- Place the casualty in the supine position.

- Raise the arm on the affected side above the casualty's head.

- Select the insertion site at the anterior axillary line over the fourth or fifth intercostal space.

- Clean the site with povidone-iodine solution.

- Put on sterile gloves.

- Drape the area.

- Liberally infiltrate the area with the 1 or 2 percent lidocaine solution and allow time for medication to take effect if patient symptoms permit.

3. Insert the tube.

- Make a 2 to 3 centimeter (cm) transverse incision over the selected site and extend it down to the intercostal muscles.

Note: The skin incision should be 1 to 2 cm below the intercostal space through which the tube will be placed.

- Insert the large forceps through the intercostal muscles in the next intercostal space above the skin incision.
- Puncture the parietal pleura with the tip of the forceps and slightly enlarge the hole by opening the clamp 1.5 to 2 cm.

> **Caution:** Avoid puncturing the lung. Always use the superior margin of the rib to avoid the intercostal nerves and vessels.

- Immediately insert a gloved finger in the incision to clear any adhesions, clots, etc.
- Grasp the tip of the chest tube with forceps. Insert the tip of the tube into the incision as you withdraw your finger.
- Advance the tube until the last side hole is 2.5 to 5 cm inside the chest wall.
- Connect the end of the tube to a one-way drainage valve (e.g., Heimlich valve or improvised).
- Secure the tube using the suture materials.
- Apply an occlusive dressing over the incision site.
- Radiograph the chest to confirm placement, if available.

4. Reassess the casualty.

- Check for bilateral breath sounds.
- Monitor and record vital signs every 15 minutes.

5. Document the procedure.

TACTICAL COMBAT CASUALTY CARE HANDBOOK

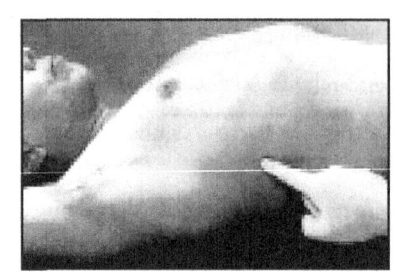

Figure 2-18. Chest tube insertion site

Section IV: Vascular Access (Addressed during Tactical Field Care and Tactical Evacuation Care Phases)

Intraosseous Placement:
First Access for Shock and Trauma (FAST1) System

Necessary equipment: FAST1 System device, 10 cubic centimeter (cc) syringe with normal saline for flush, saline lock, and tape.

1. Positioning and preparing the site.

   - The provider should position themselves above the head of the casualty to avoid improper insertion of the device.
   - Expose the sternum.
   - Identify the sternal notch (not the xyphoid process).

2. Place the target patch.

   - Remove the top half of the backing ("Remove 1") from the patch.
   - Place index finger on the sternal notch, perpendicular to the skin.
   - Align the locating notch in the target patch with the sternal notch.
   - Verify that the target zone (circular hole) of the patch is directly over the casualty's midline, and press firmly on the patch to engage the adhesive and secure the patch.
   - Remove the remaining backing ("Remove 2") and secure the patch to the casualty.

CENTER FOR ARMY LESSONS LEARNED

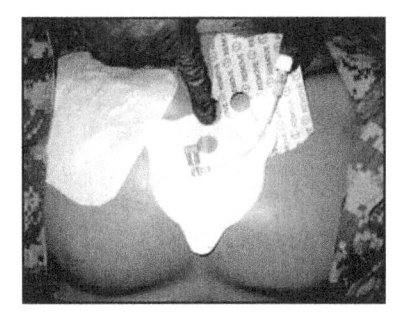

Figure 2-19. FAST1 target patch

3. Insert the introducer.

- Position yourself over the head of the patient facing toward the patient's feet.
- Remove the cap from the introducer.
- Place the bone probe cluster needles in the target zone of the target patch.
- Hold the introducer perpendicular to the skin of the casualty.
- Pressing straight along the introducer axis, with hand and elbow in line, push with a firm, constant force until a release is heard and felt.
- Expose the infusion tube by gently withdrawing the introducer. The stylet supports will fall away.

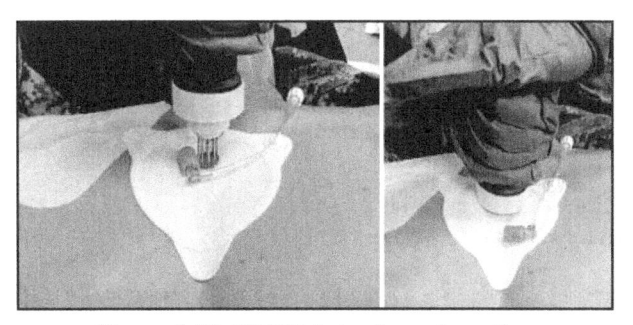

Figure 2-20. FAST1 introducer insertion

Warning: Avoid extreme force or twisting motions.

4. Connect the infusion tube.

- Connect the infusion tube to the right-angle female connector (blue tip).
- Flush catheter with 10 milliliter (mls) of sterile IV solution.
- May also add 2 to 3 mls of 2 percent lidocaine to reduce pain during infusion.
- Attach a saline lock to the remaining luer lock connector.

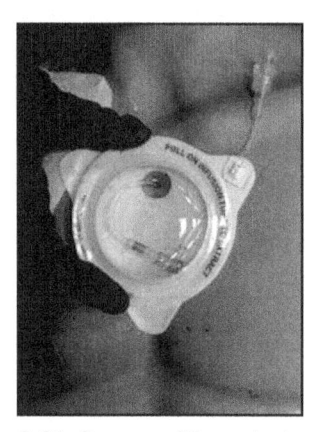

Figure 2-21. Secure with protector dome

5. Place the protector dome directly over the target patch and press firmly to engage the Velcro fastening.

6. Reinforce with tape.

Peripheral Intravascular Access

Necessary equipment: Intravenous (IV) tubing, IV fluids, 18-gauge or larger IV needle with catheter, saline lock, constricting band, antiseptic wipes, gloves, tape, and 2- x 2-inch gauze sponges.

1. Select an appropriate access site on an extremity.

- Avoid sites over joints.
- Avoid injured extremities.
- Avoid extremities with significant wounds proximal to the IV insertion site.

2. Prepare the site.

- Apply the constriction band around the limb, about 2 inches above the puncture site.
- Clean the site with antiseptic solution.

3. Put on gloves.

4. Puncture the vein.

- Stabilize skin at the puncture site with nondominant thumb, pulling the skin downward until taut. Avoid placing thumb directly over the vein to avoid collapsing.
- Position the needle point, bevel up, parallel to the vein, 1/2 inch below the venipuncture site.
- Hold the needle at a 20- to 30-degree angle and insert it through the skin.
- Move the needle forward about 1/2 inch into the vein.
- Confirm the puncture by observing blood in the flash chamber.

Note: A faint give may be felt as the needle enters the vein.

5. Advance the catheter.

- Grasp the hub and advance the needle into the vein up to the hub.

Note: This prevents backflow of blood from the hub.

- While holding the hub, press lightly on the skin with the fingers of the other hand.
- Remove the needle from the catheter and secure it in a safe place to avoid accidental needle sticks.
- Attach a saline lock, preferably needleless.

6. Connect the catheter to the IV infusion tubing. An 18-gauge needle will be required if not using a needleless saline lock.

- Begin the infusion.
- Observe the site for infiltration of fluids into the surrounding soft tissue.

7. Secure the catheter and tubing to the skin and dress the site.

Section V: Hypothermia Prevention (Addressed during Tactical Field Care and Tactical Evacuation Care Phases)

1. Stop bleeding and resuscitate appropriately. Use warm fluids if available.

2. Remove any wet clothes and replace with dry clothes, if possible.

3. Use the hypothermia prevention and management kit (HPMK).

   - Place the casualty on a Blizzard Blanket or heat-reflective shell to maintain body temperature.

   - Place a Ready-Heat blanket on the casualty's torso to aid in increasing body temperature. Do not place the Ready-Heat blanket directly on the casualty's skin, which may cause a burn.

   - Wrap the Blizzard Blanket or heat-reflective shell around the casualty. If a survival blanket of any kind is not available, then find dry blankets, poncho liners, space blankets, sleeping bags, body bags, or anything that will retain heat and keep the casualty dry.

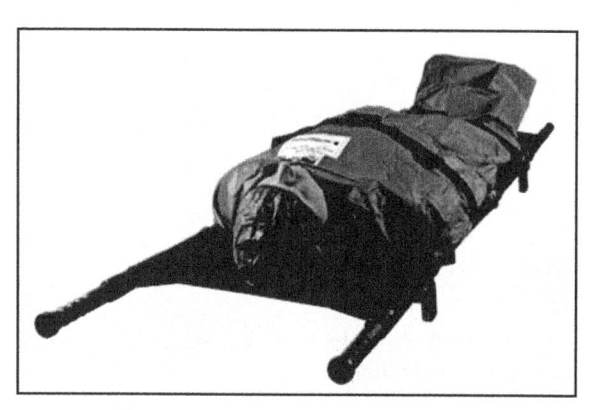

Figure 2-22. Heat Reflective Shell

Tactical Evacuation Care Phase

1. The casualty should remain wrapped in the Blizzard Survival Blanket or Heat-Reflective Shell with Ready-Heat blanket while awaiting evacuation; en route care should be provided.

2. If these items were not available in the other phases of care, check with evacuation personnel to see if they have them or any other items that can be used to prevent heat loss.

3. Wrap the casualty in dry blankets and, during helicopter transport, try to keep the wind from open doors from blowing over or under the casualty.

4. Use a portable fluid warmer on all intraosseous (IO)/IV sites and for all liquid medication administered (Hextend, Lactated Ringers, Tranexamic acid [TXA], blood, etc.). Administering cold fluids contributes to the likelihood of the casualty developing hypothermia.

Section VI: Medication Considerations

Nonsteroidal Anti-Inflammatory (NSAIDS)

The most commonly used medication that interferes with the forming of blood clots and ultimately compound bleeding belong to the cyclooxygenase-1 (COX-1) family. These medications include aspirin, ibuprofen, indomethicin, naproxen, etc. All are very common medications consumed globally by soldiers deployed to hostile fire zones. Current research supports eliminating this modifiable risk factor in an effort to reduce the difficulty of damage control resuscitation in wounded Soldiers.[1]

Endnotes

1. Harris, M., R. Baba, R. Nahouraii, et al. "Self-Induced Bleeding Diathesis in Soldiers at a FOB in South Eastern Afghanistan." *Military Medicine.* 177(8): 928-929. 2010; De La Cruz, J.P., J.J. Reyes, M.I. Ruiz-Moreno, et al. "Differences in the In Vitro Antiplatelet Effect of Dexibuprofen, Ibuprofen, and Flurbiprofen in Human Blood." *Anesthesia Analgesia.* 111(6). 1341-1346. 2010.

Appendix A

Triage Categories

Medical Evacuation in a Theater of Operations Tactics, Techniques, and Procedures, Field Manual 8-10-6, April 2000

Triage is the medical sorting of patients according to type and seriousness of injury, likelihood of survival, and the establishment of priority for treatment and/or evacuation to assure medical care is of the greatest benefit to the largest number. The categories are:

- Immediate. Those who require limited treatment and can be returned to duty. This group includes those Soldiers requiring lifesaving surgery. The surgical procedures in this category should not be time consuming and should concern only those patients with high chances of survival. Examples include:
  - Upper airway obstruction.
  - Severe respiratory distress.
  - Life-threatening bleeding.
  - Tension pneumothorax.
  - Hemothorax.
  - Flail chest.
  - Extensive 2nd- or 3rd-degree burns.
  - Untreated poisoning (chemical agent) and severe symptoms.
  - Heat stroke.
  - Decompensated shock.
  - Rapidly deteriorating level of consciousness.
  - Any other life-threatening condition that is rapidly deteriorating.

- Delayed. Patients requiring immediate care to save life or limb; This group includes those wounded who are badly in need of time-consuming surgery, but whose general condition permits delay in surgical treatment without unduly endangering life. Sustaining treatment will be required (e.g., stabilizing intravenous fluids, splinting, and administration of antibiotics, catheterization, gastric decompression, and relief of pain). Examples include:
    - Compensated shock.
    - Fracture, dislocation, or injury causing circulatory compromise.
    - Severe bleeding, controlled by a tourniquet or other means.
    - Suspected compartment syndrome.
    - Penetrating head, neck, chest, back, or abdominal injuries without airway or breathing compromise or decompensated shock.
    - Uncomplicated immobilized cervical spine injuries.
    - Large, dirty, or crushed soft-tissue injuries.
    - Severe combat stress symptoms or psychosis.
- Minimal. Patients who, after emergency treatment, incur little additional risk by delay or further treatment. These casualties have relatively minor injuries and can effectively care for themselves or can be helped by non-medical personnel. Examples include:
    - Uncomplicated closed fractures and dislocations.
    - Uncomplicated or minor lacerations (including those involving tendons, muscles, and nerves).
    - Frostbite.
    - Strains and sprains.
    - Minor head injury (loss of consciousness of less than five minutes with normal mental status and equal pupils).

- Expectant. Patients so critically injured that only complicated and prolonged treatment will improve life expectancy. Casualties in this category have wounds that are so extensive that even if they were the sole casualty and had the benefit of optimal medical resource application, their survival would be unlikely. The expectant casualty should not be abandoned, but should be separated from the view of other casualties. Using a minimal but competent staff, provide comfort measures for these casualties. Examples include:
  - Traumatic cardiac arrest.
  - Massive brain injury.
  - 2nd- or 3rd-degree burns over 70 percent of the body surface area.
  - Gunshot wound to the head with a Glasgow Coma Scale of 3.

Appendix B
Medical Evacuation Request
(9-Line and MIST Report)

Line 1. Location of the pickup site.

Line 2. Radio frequency, call sign, and suffix.

Line 3. Number of patients by precedence:

   A - Urgent
   B - Urgent Surgical
   C - Priority
   D - Routine
   E - Convenience

Line 4. Special equipment required:

   A - None
   B - Hoist
   C - Extraction equipment
   D - Ventilator

Line 5. Number of patients:

   A - Litter
   B - Ambulatory

Line 6. Security at pickup site:*

   N - No enemy troops in area
   P - Possible enemy troops in area (approach with caution)
   E - Enemy troops in area (approach with caution)
   X - Enemy troops in area (armed escort required)

*In peacetime: Number and type of wounds, injuries, and illnesses (but also desired in wartime for planning purposes).

Line 7. Method of marking pickup site:

   A - Panels
   B - Pyrotechnic signal
   C - Smoke signal
   D - None
   E - Other

Line 8. Patient nationality and status:

    A - U.S. military
    B - U.S. civilian
    C - Non-U.S. military
    D - Non-U.S. civilian
    E - Enemy prisoner of war

Line 9. Nuclear, biological, and chemical (NBC) contamination:**

    N - Nuclear
    B - Biological
    C - Chemical

**In peacetime: Terrain description of pickup site (but also desired in wartime, as NBC contamination is rarely an issue).

MIST Report

Depending on the theater of operation and aeromedical evacuation unit standard operating procedures, a MIST report may be required prior to dispatching an air ambulance for a medical evacuation. A MIST report includes the following:

- Mechanism of injury.

- Injuries sustained or illness.

- Signs and symptoms.

- Treatment rendered or required.

Appendix C
Medical Evacuation Precedence Categories

Medical Evacuation,
Field Manual 4-02.2, May 2007

The initial decision for evacuation priorities is made by the treatment element or the senior military person at the scene based on advice from medical personnel. Soldiers are evacuated by the most expeditious means of evacuation based on their medical condition, assigned evacuation precedence, and availability of medical evacuation platforms. Patients may be evacuated from the point of injury or wounding to a medical treatment facility in closest proximity to the point of injury/wounding to ensure they are stabilized to withstand the rigors of evacuation over great distances. The evacuation precedence for the U.S. Army operations at Roles 1 through 3 are:

- Priority I, URGENT is assigned to emergency cases that should be evacuated as soon as possible and within a maximum of 1 hour to save life, limb, or eyesight and to prevent complications of serious illness and to avoid permanent disability.

- Priority IA, URGENT-SURGICAL is assigned to patients who must receive far forward surgical intervention to save life and stabilize for further evacuation.

- Priority II, PRIORITY is assigned to sick and wounded personnel requiring prompt medical care. This precedence is used when the individual should be evacuated within 4 hours. Additionally, if his medical condition could deteriorate to such a degree that he will become an URGENT precedence or whose requirements for special treatment are not available locally, or who will suffer unnecessary pain or disability, the precedence is assigned as a PRIORITY.

- Priority III, ROUTINE is assigned to sick and wounded personnel requiring evacuation but whose condition is not expected to deteriorate significantly. The sick and wounded in this category should be evacuated within 24 hours.

- Priority IV, CONVENIENCE is assigned to patients for whom evacuation by medical vehicle is a matter of medical convenience rather than necessity.

CENTER FOR ARMY LESSONS LEARNED

Note: North Atlantic Treaty Organization Standard Agreement (NATO STANAG 3204) has deleted the category of Priority IV, CONVENIENCE. However, this category is still included in the U.S. Army evacuation priorities, as there is a requirement for it in the operational environment.

Appendix D
Roles of Medical Care
Army Health System, Army Tactics, Techniques, and Procedures 4-02, October 2011

The Army Medical Department is in a transitional phase with terminology. This publication makes every attempt to use the most current terminology; however, other Field Manual (FM) 4-02-series and FM 8-series may use the older terminology. Changes in terminology are a result of adopting the terminology currently used in the joint and/or North Atlantic Treaty Organization (NATO) and American, British, Canadian, Australian and New Zealand (ABCA) Armies' publication arenas. Also, the following terms are synonymous and *the current terms are listed first*:

- Roles of care, echelons of care, and level of care.

Role 1. The first medical care a Soldier receives is provided at Role 1. This role of care includes:

- Immediate lifesaving measures.
- Disease and nonbattle injury prevention.
- Combat and operational stress prevention measures.
- Patient location and acquisition (collection).
- Medical evacuation from supported units (point of injury or wounding, company-aid posts, or casualty collection points) to a higher role supporting medical treatment facilities.
- Treatment provided by combat medics or treatment squads. Major emphasis is placed on those measures necessary for the patient to return to duty or to stabilize and allow for evacuation to the next role of care. These measures include life-saving interventions such as hemorrhage control, airway and breathing emergency measures, and preventing shock.

Skill levels providing medical care at Role 1 include:

- Self-aid and/or buddy-aid. Each individual Soldier should be trained in Tactical Combat Casualty Care procedures and the lifesaving interventions that address the four preventable causes of death on the battlefield. This training enables the Soldier to implement the medical equipment provided to them in the Improved First Aid Kit (IFAK) and Warrior Aid and Litter Kit (WALK).

- Combat Lifesaver (CLS). The CLS provider is a nonmedical Soldier selected by the unit commander for additional training beyond basic first-aid procedures. A minimum on one Soldier per squad, crew, team, or equivalent-sized unit should receive CLS training and certification. The primary duty of this Soldier does not change; the additional duty as a CLS is merely to provide enhanced first-aid until the combat medic arrives, or to assist in a mass casualty scenario.

- Medical personnel. Role 1 medical treatment is provided by a combat medic, physician assistant, or physician assigned/attached to a Battalion Aid Station (BAS) medical treatment facility (MTF). The combat medic forward of a BAS is the first medically trained Soldier to provide lifesaving interventions based on military occupational specialty specific training. The licensed providers at this Role are trained and equipped to provide advanced trauma management and stabilize a combat casualty prior to evacuation to a higher role of care.

Role 2. At this role, care is rendered at the Role 2 MTF that is operated by the treatment platoon of medical companies/troops. Here, the patient is examined and his wounds and general medical condition are evaluated to determine his treatment and evacuation precedence as a single patient among other patients. Advanced trauma management and emergency medical treatment, including beginning resuscitation, is continued, and if necessary, additional emergency measures are instituted, but do not go beyond the measures dictated by immediate necessities. The Role 2 MTF has the capability to provide packed red blood cells (liquid), limited x-ray, clinical laboratory, dental support, combat operational stress control (COSC), and preventive medicine. The Role 2 MTF provides a greater capability to resuscitate trauma patients than is available at Role 1. Those patients who can return to duty within 72 hours (one to three days) are held for treatment.

Patients who are non-transportable due to their medical condition may require resuscitative surgical care from a forward surgical team collocated with a medical company/troop. (A discussion of the forward surgical team is contained in FM 4-02.25.) This role of care provides medical evacuation from Role 1 MTFs and also provides Role 1 medical treatment on an area support basis for units without organic Role 1 resources. Army Health System (AHS) assets are located in the:

- Medical company (brigade support battalion), assigned to modular brigades, which include the heavy brigade combat team, infantry brigade combat team, the Stryker brigade combat team, and the medical troop in the armored cavalry regiment.
- Medical company (area support) that is an echelon above brigade asset provides direct support to the modular division and support to echelons above brigade units.

Note: The Role 2 definition used by NATO forces (Allied Joint Publication-4.10[A]) includes the following terms and descriptions not used by U.S. Army forces. U.S. Army forces subscribe to the basic definition of a Role 2 MTF providing greater resuscitative capability than is available at Role 1. It does not subscribe to the interpretation that a surgical capability is mandatory at this Role. The NATO descriptions are:

- A medical company with a collocated forward surgical team may be referred to as a *light maneuver* Role 2 facility.
- An enhanced Role 2 MTF may be used in stability operations scenarios and consists of the medical company, forward surgical team, and other specialty augmentation as deemed appropriate by the situation. Specialty augmentation is only provided when the situation has stabilized and it is not anticipated that the enhanced MTF will be required to relocate.

Role 3. These patients are treated in an MTF that is staffed and equipped to provide care to all categories of patients, to include resuscitation, initial wound surgery, damage control surgery, and postoperative treatment. This role of care expands the support provided at Role 2. Patients who are unable to tolerate and survive movement over long distances receive surgical care in a hospital as close to the supported unit as the tactical situation allows. This role includes provisions for:

- Evacuating patients from supported units.
- Providing care for all categories of patients in a MTF with the proper staff and equipment.
- Providing support on an area basis to units without organic medical assets.

Role 4. This medical care is found in the continental U.S. military hospitals and other overseas safe havens. Mobilization requires expansion of military hospital capacities and the inclusion of Department of Veterans Affairs and civilian hospital beds in the National Disaster Medical System to meet the increased demands created by the evacuation of patients from the areas of operation. These hospitals represent the most definitive medical care available within the AHS.

Appendix E
Combat Wound Pack

Contents:

1. Meloxicam (Mobic), 15 milligrams (mg) x 1 per oral (PO).

2. Acetaminophen (Tylenol), 650 mg caplet x 2 PO.

3. Moxifloxicin, 400 mg x 1.

Instructions: In the event of an open combat wound and the Soldier is still able to continue to fight, swallow all the pills in the pack with water.

Note: Soldiers should be instructed in the use of the combat wound pack and should be issued the pack prior to combat.

Warning: Do not issue the wound pack to Soldiers with known drug allergies to any of the components. In these cases it will be necessary to replace the contents with appropriate substitutes.

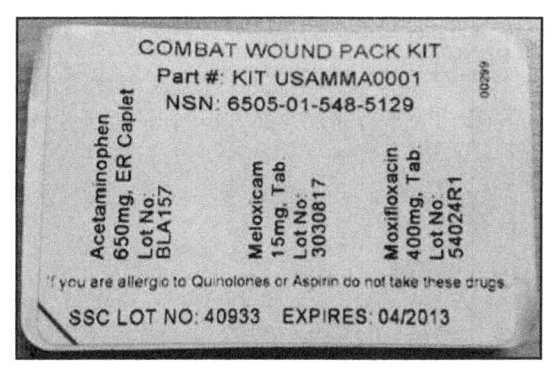

Figure E-1. Combat wound pack

Appendix F
Improved First Aid Kit

The Improved First Aid Kit (IFAK) is a rapid-fielding initiative item, issued to deploying units by the unit's central issue facility.

Contents:

- Nasopharyngeal airway.
- Exam gloves (4).
- 2-inch tape.
- Trauma dressing.
- Kerlix (compressed gauze bandage rolls).
- Combat application tourniquet.
- Modular lightweight load-carrying equipment pouch with retaining lanyard.
- The IFAK is augmented aftermarket with the following items:
    - Combat Gauze (Per All Army Activities [ALARACT] 185/2005).
    - Department of Army Form 7656 (Per Army Regulation 40-66 and ALARACTs 355/2009 and 10-2010).

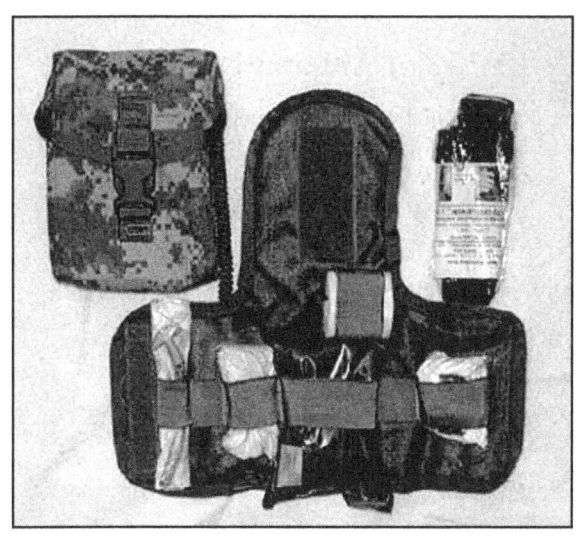

Figure F-1. Improved First Aid Kit (IFAK)
NSN: 6545-01-530-0929

Appendix G
Warrior Aid and Litter Kit

The following items are included as components of the Warrior Aid and Litter Kit (WALK):

- 1 x bag (WALK).
- 10 x gloves (trauma, nitrile, Black Talon [5 pair]).
- 2 x nasopharyngeal airway (28 French with lubricant).
- 2 x gauze (Petrolatum 3" x 18").
- 2 x needle/catheter (14 gauge x 3.25").
- 2 x combat application tourniquet.
- 6 x trauma dressing.
- 4 x gauze (compressed, vacuum-sealed).
- 1 x emergency trauma abdominal dressing.
- 2 x SAM II splint.
- 1 x shears (trauma, 7.25").
- 2 x tape (surgical, adhesive 2").
- 1 x card (reference, combat casualty).
- 2 x card (individual, combat casualty).
- 1 x panel (recognition, orange).
- 1 x litter (evacuation platform, Talon 90C).
- 1 x hypothermia prevention and management kit.
- 4 x strap (tie down, universal litter).

Note: There should be a WALK on every vehicle in a convoy.

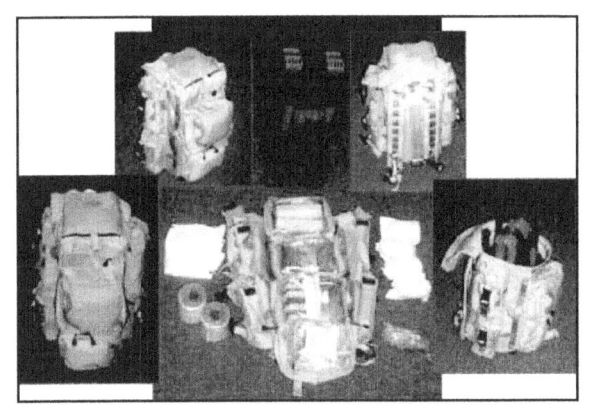

Figure G-1. WALK, National Stock Number: 6545-01-532-4962

Appendix H
Aid Bag Considerations

There is not a standard packing list for an aid bag. The contents of a tactical provider's aid bag are dependent upon:

- The skill level of the tactical provider.
- The type of mission.
- The length of mission.

The overall approach is not the packing of a single aid bag, but developing a tiered approach and supplying it with appropriate levels of medical supplies to meet the challenges in the different phases of care. Tactical Combat Casualty Care, and the supplies that facilitate that care, start with each Soldier's improved first aid kit and increase in application and amount to meet mission requirements and any worst-case scenario. Attempts should be made to pack the aid bags and stage them appropriately. The specific types and amount of medical supplies in the proper location will ensure success.

Appendix I
National Stock Numbers

Equipment	National Stock Number
Airway Supplies	
Nasopharyngeal Airway	6515-00-300-2900
King LT	Size 3: 6515-01-515-0146 Size 4: 6515-01-515-0151 Size 5: 6515-01-515-0161
Emergency Cricothyrotomy Kit	6515001-573-0692
Breathing Supplies	
Bolin Chest Seal	6501-01-549-0939
HALO Chest Seal	6515-01-532-8019
Needle Decompression (14 gauge x 3.25")	6515-01-541-0635
Circulation (Hemorrhage) Supplies	
Combat Application Tourniquet	6515-01-521-7976
Special Operations Forces Tactical Tourniquet	6515-01-530-7015
Combat Gauze	6510-01-562-3325
H&H Compressed Bandage Gauze (IFAK)	6510-01-503-2117
Combat Ready Clamp	6515-01-589-9135
Junctional Emergency Treatment Tool	6515-01-616-5841
The "H" Bandage	6510-01-540-6484
The Emergency Bandage (IFAK)	6510-01-460-0849

Vascular Access/Fluids	
FAST1 IO System	6515-01-453-0960
EZ IO Driver	6515-01-537-9615
EZ IO Driver Needle Sets	6515-01-537-9007 (Tibial) 6515-01-577-0312 (Humeral Head) 6515-01-518-8497 (Pediatric)
EZ IO Manual Needle Set	6515-01-540-9794 (Tibial, non-sternal)
Hetastarch (Hextend) 500 ml	6505-01-498-8636
Tactical IV Starter Kit	6515-01-587-5717
Hypothermia Prevention	
Hypothermia Prevention and Management Kit (Includes Heat Reflective Shell & Ready Heat)	6515-01-532-8056
Blizzard Survival Blanket	6532-01-534-6932
Ready-Heat Blanket	6532-01-525-4062
Miscellaneous Supplies	
Sked Basic Rescue System	6530-01-260-1222
Warrior Aid & Litter Kit	6545-01-587-1199
Improved First Aid Kit	6545-01-532-4962
Talon II Model 90C	6530-01-504-9051
Combat Lifesaver Kit	6515-01-494-1951
Combat Eye Shield	6515-01-590-2668
Combat Pill Pack	6505-01-548-5129
Sam Pelvic Sling II	6515-01-509-6866

Appendix J
References and Resources

Allen, P.B., S.W. Salyer, M.A. Dubick, et al. "Preventing Hypothermia: Comparison of Current Devices Used by the U.S. Army in an In Vitro Warmed Fluid Model." *Journal of Trauma.* 69(1): S154-S161, 2010.

Arishita, G.I., J.S. Vayer, and R.F. Bellamy. "Cervical Spine Immobilization of Penetrating Neck Wounds in a Hostile Environment." *Journal of Trauma.* 1989, 29: 1453–1454.

Bellamy, R.F. "The Causes of Death in Conventional Land Warfare: Implications for Combat Casualty Care Research." *Military Medicine.* 149:55, 1984.

Bottlang, M., J.C. Krieg, M. Mohr, et al. "Emergent Management of Pelvic Ring Fractures with use of Circumferential Compression." *Journal of Bone and Joint Surgery.* 84(A) Suppl. 2002.

Butler, F. "Fluid Resuscitation in Tactical Combat Casualty Care: Brief History and Current Status." *Journal of Trauma.* 70(5).2011.

Butler, F. "Tactical Combat Casualty Care: Update 2009." *Journal of Trauma.* 691(1). S10-S13. 2010.

Butler, F.K. "Tactical Combat Casualty Care: Combining Good Medicine with Good Tactics." *Journal of Trauma.* 54: 2003.

Butler, F.K. Jr., J. Hagmann, and E.G. Butler. "Tactical Combat Casualty Care in Special Operations." *Military Medicine.*161, Suppl.: 3–16, 1996.

De La Cruz, J.P., J.J. Reyes, M.I. Ruiz-Moreno, et al. "Differences in the In Vitro Antiplatelet Effect of Dexibuprofen, Ibuprofen, and Flurbiprofen in Human Blood." *Anesthesia Analgesia.* 111(6). 1341-1346. 2010.

Dubick, M.A. and J.F. Kragh. "Evaluation of the Combat Ready Clamp to Control Bleeding in Human Cadavers, Manikins, Swine Femoral Artery Hemorrhage Model and Swine Carcasses." U.S. Army Institutional Report. June 2012.

DuBose, J., G.R. Teixeira, P. Hadjizacharia, et al. "The Role of Routine Spinal and Immobilization in Asymptomatic Patients after Gunshot Wounds." *Injury.* 40(8), 860-863. 2009.

Eastridge, B.J., R.L. Mabry, P. Seguin, et al. "Death on the Battlefield (2001-2011): Implications for the Future of Combat Casualty Care." *Journal of Trauma.* 73(6) Suppl.: 5. 2012.

Harcke, H.T., L.A. Pearse, A.D. Levy, J.M. Getz, and S.R. Robinson. "Chest Wall Thickness in Military Personnel: Implications for Needle Thoracentesis in Tension Pneumothorax." *Military Medicine*. 172: 1260-1263. 2007.

Harris, M., R. Baba, R. Nahouraii, et al. "Self-Induced Bleeding Diathesis in Soldiers at a FOB in South Eastern Afghanistan." *Military Medicine*. 177(8): 928-929. 2010.

Hospenthal, D.R., C.K. Murray, R.C. Anderson, et al. "Guidelines for the Prevention of Infections Associated with Combat-Related Injuries: 2011 Update." *Journal of Trauma*. 71(2) Suppl. 2011.

Inaba, K., B.C. Branco, M. Eckstein, et al. "Optimal Positioning for Emergent Needle Thoracostomy: A Cadaver-based Study. *Journal of Trauma*. 71(5). 1099-1103. 2011.

Kotwal, R., K. O'Connor, J. Holcomb, et al. "A Novel Pain Management Strategy for Combat Casualty Care." *Annals of Emergency Medicine*. 44: 121-127.2004.

Kragh, J.F., M.L. Littrel, J.A. Jones, et al. "Battle Casualty Survival with Emergency Tourniquet Use to Stop Limb Bleeding." *Journal of Emergency Medicine*. 41(6): 590-597.

Kragh, J.F., M.L. O'Neill, T.J. Walters, et al. "The Military Emergency Tourniquet Program's Lessons Learned with Devices and Designs." *Military Medicine*. 176:10, 1144, 2011.

Kragh, J.F., T.J. Walters, D.G. Baer, et al. "Survival with Emergency Tourniquet Use to Stop Bleeding in Major Limb Trauma." *Annals of Surgery*. 249 (1): 1–7, 2009.

McKay, S., D. Callaway. *Rounding out the Warrior, Part II: Assault Rescue: Point of Wounding Extraction*. National Officers Tactical Association.

McKeague, A.L. "Evaluation of Patient Active Warming Systems." Military Health System Research Symposium, Tactical Combat Casualty Care breakout session. Ft. Lauderdale, FL. August 2012.

McManus, J., A.L. Yerhov, and D. Ludwig. "Radial Pulse Character Relationships to Systolic Blood Pressure and Trauma Outcomes." *Prehospital Emergency Care*. 9(4). 423-428.

Morrison, C.A., M.M. Carrick, M.A. Norman, et al. "Hypotensive Resuscitation Strategy Reduces Transfusion Requirements and Severe Postoperative Coagulopathy in Trauma Patients with Hemorrhagic Shock: Preliminary Results of a Randomized Controlled Trial." *Journal of Trauma*. 70(3): 652-663, 2011.

Mott, J.C. *Prehospital Trauma Life Support Manual: Tactical Emergency Medical Support, 8th ed.* Ch. 23. Jones and Bartlett. In Press.

Otten, M. "Management of Open Sucking Chest Wounds." Committee on Tactical Combat Casualty Care (TCCC) meeting proposed Tactical Combat Casualty Care Guideline Change. 24 July 2008.

Rosemary, A.S., P.A. Norris, S.M. Olson, et al. "Prehospital Traumatic Cardiac Arrest: The Cost of Futility." *Journal of Trauma.* 38: 468–474, 1998.

Rush, S. "Cadaver Lab Training for Humeral Head IO Insertion." Military Health System Research Symposium. August 2013.

Stockinger, Z.T. and N.E. McSwain. "Additional Evidence in Support of Withholding or Terminating Cardiopulmonary Resuscitation for Trauma Patients in the Field." *Journal of the American College of Surgeons.* 198(2), 227-231. 2004.

Stuke, L.E., P.T. Pons, J.S. Guy, et al. "Prehospital Spine Immobilization for Penetrating Trauma: Review and Recommendations from the Prehospital Trauma Life Support Executive Committee." *Journal of Trauma.* 71(3), 2011.

U.S. Army Institute of Surgical Research. *Joint Theater Trauma System Clinical Practice Guidelines: Fresh Whole Blood Transfusion.* October 2012.

Resources

Bond, C. (2010). *68W Advanced Field Craft: Combat Medic Skills. American Association of Orthopedic Surgeons.* Sudbury, MA: Jones and Bartlett.

Department of Defense (2004). *Emergency War Surgery. 3rd Revision.* Borden Institute.

National Association of Emergency Medical Technicians (2013). *Prehospital Trauma Life Support Manual, Military 8th edition.* Excelsier.

Soldier Training Publication 8-68W13-SM-TG (2009). *Soldier's Manual and Trainer's Guide: MOS 68W, Health Care Specialist.*

Center for Army Lessons Learned (CALL) Newsletter 04-18, *Medical Planning.*

CALL Special Edition 05-8, *Deploying Health Care Provider.*

Online Resources

U.S. Army Medical Department (AMEDD) Center and School Portal, Deployment Relevant Training: https://www.cs.amedd.army.mil/deployment2.aspx.

AMEDD Lessons Learned: http://lessonslearned.amedd.army.mil.

CALL: <http://call.army.mil/.

Center for Pre-Deployment Medicine: Tactical Combat Medical Care Course: https://www.us.army.mil/suite/page/312889.

TACTICAL COMBAT CASUALTY CARE HANDBOOK

Military Review (MR)

MR is a revered journal that provides a forum for original thought and debate on the art and science of land warfare and other issues of current interest to the U.S. Army and the Department of Defense. Find MR at <http://usacac.army.mil/cac2/militaryreview/index.asp>.

TRADOC Intelligence Support Activity (TRISA)

TRISA is a field agency of the TRADOC G2 and a tenant organization on Fort Leavenworth. TRISA is responsible for the development of intelligence products to support the policy-making, training, combat development, models, and simulations arenas. Find TRISA Threats at <https://dcsint-threats.leavenworth.army.mil/default.aspx> (requires AKO password and ID).

Combined Arms Center-Capability Development Integration Directorate (CAC-CDID)

CAC-CDIC is responsible for executing the capability development for a number of CAC proponent areas, such as Information Operations, Electronic Warfare, and Computer Network Operations, among others. CAC-CDID also teaches the Functional Area 30 (Information Operations) qualification course. Find CAC-CDID at <http://usacac.army.mil/cac2/cdid/index.asp>.

Army Irregular Warfare Fusion Cell (AIWFC)

AIWFC integrates and collaborates information exchange and analysis for irregular warfare (IW) activities in order to advocate DOTMLPF (doctrine, organization, training, materiel, leadership and education, personnel, and facilities) solutions addressing IW threats. AIWFC synchronizes and assists in the development of IW and countering irregular threats enterprises to support a coherent Army strategy that accounts for building partner capacity, stability operations, and the integration of unconventional warfare and counterterrorism. Find AIWFC at: <http://usacac.army.mil/cac2/AIWFC>.

Joint Center for International Security Force Assistance (JCISFA)

JCISFA's mission is to capture and analyze security force assistance (SFA) lessons from contemporary operations to advise combatant commands and military departments on appropriate doctrine; practices; and proven tactics, techniques, and procedures (TTP) to prepare for and conduct SFA missions efficiently. JCISFA was created to institutionalize SFA across DOD and serve as the DOD SFA Center of Excellence. Find JCISFA at <https://jcisfa.jcs.mil/Public/Index.aspx>.

Support CAC in the exchange of information by telling us about your successes so they may be shared and become Army successes.

Made in the USA
Middletown, DE
29 June 2020